The Five Day Dissertation

CHARLIE FREEMAN BA.(HONS)

ISBN: 1516956044
ISBN-13: 9781516956043

CONTENTS

CHAPTER 1
INTRODUCTION

Whenever you find yourself on the side of the majority, it is time to pause and reflect.
- MARK TWAIN

JUNE 27th

The page loaded slowly, Jay checked his results first on his aging laptop. Waiting with baited breath, he clicked through to 'dissertation'…

67.78%. A high 2:1.

'Oh my god we did it... A TWO ONE!' Jay reiterated loudly.

Emboldened, I signed on. Jay may have done it, but for all my confidence, mine could still come out as a third. For the time I'd spent on it, it probably should.

I clicked through to 'dissertation' and felt my own relief, also a high 2:1.

It is a rare thing to achieve over 67% in your dissertation. Even rarer still were Jay and I. I'd spent a fraction of the time on mine, and after refining the processes, Jay even shorter. I'd taught him in just five days.

Over a beer, we discussed the possibilities.

'You could hold lectures *here*, on dissertation productivity', Jay said, leaning back and making the stiff metal of the student union chair creak.

'Teach other students to do the same?'

'Yeah why not? You managed to teach me....'

And so the 5 day dissertation was born.

April 19th. Two months previous and six days to deadline.

I was on my third lap of the library's I.T department. It was past midnight and everyone was hunched over computers, pallid faces lit up with dark noise cancelling headphones blocking out the world, oblivious to my wandering. Every seat was taken, most dissertations were due in at the end of the week, with some 'lucky' fellows still having two to complete it.

I found Jay sitting two chairs in from the corner, one empty energy drink can crumpled on his desk, another just opened in his left hand while his right hand feverishly clicked from article to article.

'How'd it go?'

Jay turned and for a split second his face shone with terror mixed with the frustration. Reading academic articles for eight straight hours hadn't been kind to him. When he saw it was me, he relaxed, reassured his dissertation marker hadn't taken it upon himself to find him at 2am and begin marking him early.

'I have to start almost from scratch, I'm going to fail', he sighed.

'How?' I was genuinely surprised, 'You went to every tutor meeting for months!'

'Yeah, tell me about it. She went over my dissertation like I asked and it wasn't even at a third. I'm just not good at this, I can make it up with my exams - hopefully. You can't be at 50% yet either'

'Mine's finished and preliminarily marked, I'm getting a high 2:1'

'Are you kidding? How? Didn't you start like a week ago?'

'Do you want some help?'

'*Hell* yes'

Jay was right and he wasn't. I **had** started my dissertation a week previously, but I had been sourcing the correct techniques of productivity for months, from high achieving ex-students and writers.

So I started a class, lecturing to friends at first, then friend's family members going into third year, then to friends of friends until I didn't know who I was lecturing to. I had, without knowing it, began compiling all the methods it had taken these guys years to figure out, me months to compile, and Jake and the others 5 days to learn and successfully use.

Sourcing the techniques and gathering them is the hard part, learning them is the easy part. I recommend having this book open and referring back to it often.

Why this book?

While researching a method to help create a killer dissertation, I sampled almost everything that was possibly available. They were, quite simply, about as interesting to read as a set of Ikea instructions on a complicated piece of furniture. The top selling book on dissertation writing is dense to read and repeats itself often. This book is condensed to include the maximum amount of information in as easy to understand a format of possible, in order for you to easily assimilate the information and convert it into a dissertation that will crush it.

This book offers tips for both Undergraduate (BA) and Master's (MA) dissertations. This is due to the gap between these levels shrinking. Why? - The changing nature of the students in such courses. Simply put, there are now more MA students coming from other areas of study who don't have solid background knowledge in the subject. MA students also tend to be more heavily specialised in a niche area of a given subject, however, this does not pose a problem as throughout this we're focusing on productivity no matter the subject.

Our Motto: Keep Winning Small

Many small wins equate to a big win, namely a polished and presentable dissertation in a fraction of the time usually assigned to it. Maybe you're literally following the principles of this book in order to complete your dissertation in five days, maybe you're reading it in advance in order to become more efficient. Either way, writing a dissertation in five days need not be hard, but we need to be committed. Small wins keep this morale up and help us to continue pushing through.

We will complete a certain section in a **specific order** and leave it completed. Then we will move on to the next, completely ignoring all other sections until our new section is completed. It might sound the opposite, but it is psychologically proven that small wins (in this case a completed section, for example chapter one) will make you more likely to continue on the path and, ultimately, be successful overall.

We are going to follow a tried and tested format that will present your information in a clear manner, while being extremely simple to follow. This is **guaranteed** to acquire you good results if followed correctly.

CHAPTER 2
WHAT IS A DISSERTATION?

Understanding the different types of dissertation

To make things simple, we will put dissertations into two distinct categories:

Collecting your own data
Using other peoples data

The nitty-gritty of this is that tutors sometimes describe dissertations differently. Some academics call data collection dissertations 'Empirical', or 'Practical' and others using speculative data 'theoretical'.

We **are not** going to collect data if we can help it, so you won't be required to carry out experimental research to either confirm or disprove something. Don't forget, even your dissertation is focused on using collected data, you are still going need a sound theoretical basis (a strong argument) on which to base your work.

I suggest a mainly theoretical approach as it simply takes **less time** directly compared to a gathering data approach, especially as so much research has been carried out in almost every subject under the sun that it's quite easy to find articles, websites, books and essays on almost any genre and subject within it. You can make your dissertation more practical by simply **using it and quoting it**.

A theoretical study can be quite **abstract** with an emphasis on one or two issues, it's good to be abstract as there is no 'definitive' answer for the argument we will choose to explore. And so you cannot be marked down for a 'wrong' answer. In finding a question, it is common to concentrate mainly on one aspect of these issues. A list of good ones to choose for example in the humanities department are below, what takes your fancy?

Philosophical
Ethical
Cultural
Gender
Sexuality
Economic
Politics

If you do choose Empirical, the collection of data will be off of your own back, although for kicks and completely at random, an example of two ideas could be:

Gathering views of students political views, with a note of their social class.
Collecting data on how many chocolate bars are

sold at major retailers in the run after a large marketing campaign.

This data could be collected by questionnaires, observations or interviews. The data you can collect is only limited by your imagination, however as this book is for productivity and completing your dissertation in the shortest time possible, we will focus on **not gathering data.**

(If you truly have five days to complete your dissertation and you are creating a dissertation based on your own collected data, I'm not your tutor here, you will not have much choice but to **make it up.** This happens in a huge number of dissertations where the experiment didn't go to plan or the study was too difficult to actually carry out. Use the tips outlined later in the book for chapter writing to help you have a clear idea of what you want your data to say while still being plausible, and be sure to include **outliers**.)

So, theoretical dissertations will need to flow through different theories and arguments throughout their entirety. We will be using passages from many different sources to explore concepts we ourselves put forward. This need not be difficult, if we have <u>concept A</u> and <u>concept B</u>, we will simply be drawing parallels between them, finding differences, then drawing parallels. It's a zig-zag approach that keeps a solid line of argument.

<u>Looking at a dissertation first</u>

The problem many students face when writing a dissertation is the fact that they do not happen to have a dissertation to hand when writing their own, yet, a great way of easing yourself into dissertation writing is looking at some examples of previous students' work.

Where are you supposed to get these? In my experience they are rather hard to come by, if you can, ask your tutor if it's possible to get your hands on one written on a subject near your own. At the end of this book is a full dissertation for the course English Literature BA honours, at the grade of 2:1, in case you cannot get your hands on one. It is on the subject of 'chivalry' as discussed earlier, and may be a dense read, I would suggest skimming it as reading it fully will likely be intimidating at first and worse, very boring. Focus on the structures within it. I will dissect some parts of it later in the book.

If you can, get a handle on different concepts by getting access to and comparing several dissertations at the same time. Again, just to skim, you don't have time to read them all. Did you like the font? Use it for your own. Good chapter titles? Replace words but keep the sentence for your own. Great quote?

Use it or use something similar from the source, the bibliography and footnotes will lead you there.

Many successful dissertations are highly specialised, you may think explaining your subject area broadly will give you more to write about, but many times it's the opposite. Take note of the dissertation included within this book, at first, the concept of chivalry was to be explored in just one saga of books, niche enough right? No, it was too broad. In narrowing it down to just one or two characters within those books (and mostly one) gave the question a firmer more defined focus.

Play your strengths

Many people are caught up in improving their weaknesses when approaching challenging situations, whereas the most successful people tend to play on their strengths. This is true of life and in your dissertation.

In your entire life and not just in your academic experience, too often you can separate your life into sections and think of skills as tied to particular activities or times rather than being tied to you personally.

One student I interviewed was really no writer; he struggled with theoretical concepts on his dissertation on sports nutrition. He was however quite a good mathematician but did not see how he could apply this to his work. After all, writing is quite different to math.

After a chat with me, he decided to shift his entire focus to figures. He had no skill with complex wording and sentences, just figures he derived from data that was easily accessible to him in the online library.

Simple to read, but not lazily done, his logical dissertation got him a 2:1. He didn't collect data himself, just used data on his subject from valid studies. He didn't try to dance around his theory with complexity, but by playing to his strengths with figures. If stuck, or in doubt, **simplify**. You can build complexity later.

CHAPTER 3
FINDING AN INSPIRING RESEARCH QUESTION FOR YOUR DISSERTATION
(And coming up with a title that's short, clear and informative)

A good quote from Dr. Carrie Winstanley, lecturer at Roehampton University, on dissertation subject matter is:

'an undergraduate dissertation is not expected to be highly original and if your topic is close to other recent studies in the field at least you know that what you've chosen has some currency and relevance.'

I'll repeat that, *'not expected to be highly original'*.

Do not spend four weeks trying to find your perfect subject and title like many students do. You may not absolutely love your subject, if you do - great, you're ahead of 98% of everyone else.

This is a piece of work and not a lifelong career, take it from me, two months after you've handed it in you will barely remember the title. That said, enjoyment and some enthusiasm make your writing not only better quality, but faster, both of which are our aim.

For example, take a look at our theoretical concepts, what takes your fancy out of those? If you can find something that excites you even slightly you are on the fast track to success.

Avid feminist? Easy choice, explore **gender roles**. Budding politician? **Political views** and **class divides**. Cultural or economic? *All* of these concepts will have been explored to some degree in almost every area, take advantage of it.

(Alright, *yawn*, I get it, none of these subjects may be your idea of a white knuckle ride, but what if you were exploring them in a subject that you **really** enjoyed? You can derive some fun from it. Although anyone who says they enjoyed every moment of writing their 15,000 word dissertation could be a psychopath.)

How about:

The presentation of class divides in Tupac's first album?

Feminine power in 'Gossip Girl'?

Exploring parallels with Christianity and Force users in Star Wars?

Geographical nativity of famous rock climbers?

The rise of search engine optimization in the wake of Google's expansion?

How learning programming is similar to Japanese?

How immigration is affecting fashion choice in a

certain geographical location?

You may even find that as you put pen to paper (or fingers to keyboard), your dissertation evolves into something more specialised, if you can write about it, keep going, alter your question as you go. (Even alter your hypothesis or abstract when we get to it, whatever will create a more polished final product).

Any inherent bias you may have toward any particular subject needs to be withheld, (you may not even know you feel a particular way about a subject until you start writing) work solely on the evidence presented in front of you, or rather that **you** present.
Come across analytical and not prone to any assumptions. Whether you are a left wing hippie movement advocate or Neo-Nazi it's best not to state how you feel personally, it won't do you any favours. (And perhaps get some help).

The next step is in confirming that your idea is clear. What is your topic in **one sentence**? Two at the most. If you can do that without putting yourself to sleep you are onto a winner.

Here comes actual depth, and the planning stages of your chapters that will go with the structure we will outline soon.

Create Sub-Questions

You can do this by coming up with every sub-question that you think you're going to need to answer as part of your broader research question.

The more questions the better, put down all the 'what', 'why', 'when', 'where' and 'how' questions you can that relate you your title. These will, when writing, morph into meaningful sentences without you having to pause and think.

It should be clear beforehand what information readers will be gleaning from your dissertation. **Clarity is king** in terms of your title, it will help you as well as your marker, ambiguousness we will save for inside. It may also help to narrow down your title by looking at these interpretations of academic writing, you could be:

Describing something: Using your various sources to create a precise interpretation of a thing.
Explaining something: Finding patterns, relationships and occurrences. Giving an educated opinion on why these exist.
Exploring something: Gathering specifics and giving a new opinion on something.

We will be combining all of these approaches in order to make a well-rounded dissertation, but you can choose one or two to highlight and concentrate on more fully.

CHAPTER 4
RULES TO WORK BY FOR MAXIMUM EFFICIENCY

Being Effective vs. Being Efficient

Let's say you have four months to write your dissertation, you spend months gathering data that you may or may not use, months writing and editing.

We would call that being **effective**. You are moving (slowly) toward your goal, a finished and (hopefully) high quality work.
The problem is, it is not **efficient**. It is not an **economical use** of your time.

Most people when writing their dissertations or essays get by merely being **effective** and not **efficient.**

If you are the best cold-calling salesperson, you are **efficient,** you are fantastic at selling to people on the phone without misusing your time. However, you are terribly **ineffective**. You would sell x10 more through a direct or emailing list, in a fraction of the time and effort. This also works the other way, the top phone salesman is ahead of the top door to door salesman as he is more **effective** in his work.

Let's say you are fantastic at sourcing great articles and building an elaborate folder system for later use. My friend was an expert at this, until he came to write his piece and had to spend time searching through a maze of his own creation before delving into the articles and trying to find the quote he was looking for.

Here's the kicker: *Doing something unimportant well does not make it important.* On top of this, just *because something requires a lot of time does not make it important.*

Doing less of this work is not laziness. From school, college and even in the wider working world, we are taught that if we're sacrificing personal time we are being productive when in reality that's far from the truth. If you look around and see everyone whittling time away realise this, if inefficient, being busy is a form of laziness—idle thinking and indecisive action.

Maybe your parents used to think that if you were sitting with homework in front of you then you were learning, even if you were simply staring at a blank page imagining Spiderman or doodling hearts. Maybe your year 5 math teacher used to think that simply reciting times tables over and over again would through magical osmosis write them into your head. Now, thankfully, we know better.

Doing less meaningless work, so that you can focus on things of greater importance, is NOT laziness. This is hard for most to accept, because our culture tends to reward personal sacrifice instead of personal productivity.

I have met almost no first class students that actually measure the results of their actions in time, and therefore can measure contribution accurately. Luckily for us, we have five days, and so we cannot afford to be in-effective. We have to focus on being productive instead of just busy. In essence, **what** we do is much more important than **how** we do it.

Pareto's Principle

Also known as the 80/20 principle, Pareto stated that 80% of results come from 20% of inputs. Originally it was used for economics, being that 80% of wealth came from and was owned by 20% of the population, it came to be applied in many other alternative ways - from his garden peas, 20% of plants came to produce 80% of peas, to being used to measure wider social issues.
We will use his law as follows:

80% of our results come from 20% of our time and effort.

Use when needed

Many students will come up with a completed proposal many months before the deadline date. They will walk out of their tutor meeting and bee-line straight for the library, head held high, and proceed to pick out as many books relevant to their chosen topic as possible. They will then spend a few days reading, and none of this information will make it into their final dissertation because it is months before any actual writing is done. Information glanced over and not to be used until writing begins. This is **wasted time.** I know, I did the same before realising there had to be a better way.

Whatever you get out to read, you are not going to remember it in one to three months, when you are actually **writing** your dissertation. It may sound strange, but tutors can't mark you on how much you **actually** read or how good your intentions were. They will mark you solely on **what is presented in front of them**. For this reason we are going to approach this in a fashion that makes the final product excellent, without the months of wasted time.

The five month dissertation

Hannah put her head in her hands, sat at her desk in the waning hours, her dissertation was due in three weeks and she'd not even finished her first chapter. *'How is this happening?'* She said to herself,

'I've been planning and researching for months!'

She pushed away the textbooks nearest to her, towering over and suffocating her workspace. Over 20 books she had out from the library and some bought from the university shop. Their multi-coloured tabs, from hundreds of bookmarked pages, created a coral like structure either side of her. She cracked, knowing about the productivity lecture I held on Tuesdays, she sent me an e-mail exasperatingly explaining where she was at, basically, feeling like giving up.

In reality, this is a common problem, it stems from usually well achieving students suffering from over-complication and overwhelm when we have too much time to fill.

Parkinson's Law

'A task will swell in complexity in order to fill the time allotted to it' – Cyril Northcote Parkinson, English Writer.

Maybe you bought this book because you are an avid last minuter, like me or Jay from chapter one. If so, you already have experience with this. How else is it that we can complete an essay in one frenzied all-nighter and get the same if not better marks than someone who has laboured for two weeks on it?

If you only have one night, you are likely to find the time to be massively more productive -this is **Parkinson's law**.

Hannah's long timeframe had caused her work to expand to the point of infinity, if she'd had another 6 month's she'd have done another 6 months of mostly unnecessary work. That's why she was in such a state with a thousand different quotes on her desk looming, now each a piece in an infinitely complex puzzle. Where does that piece go? Now I need that piece, where did I put it?

This is where we will exceed, if you have five days, and you follow the principles of productivity in this book, you will excel.

This can apply even if you have five months to complete your dissertation, you can be much more productive even when faced with the looming prospect of another 10,000 words complete with references and sources if you **start** your session with the one thing that will make the most impact if you complete it.

Don't multi-task

Women can multi-task but men can't, it's a gender thing. - If you believe that, you'll believe anything. The truth is, sorry ladies, **no one can multi-task**. At least if you want to do something well.

You're writing, want to research a quote, you get caught up clicking on some article about the author, the next moment you're learning about what people are up to on Facebook then reading a dumb article beginning with 'you'll never believe..' and finally doing a quiz to find out which friends character you are.

Keep **FOCUSED:**

Focus
On
One
Course
Of
Action
Until
Success

I know, *profound*, but if we follow it – I mean *really* follow it. The results can be fantastic.

Our first **FOCUS** we will be working on in the next chapter is page and chapter outlines.

CHAPTER 5
TRIPLE YOUR DAILY WORDCOUNT

Write more words than you could imagine in one day

We will not be advocates of the **results-by-time-spent** approach. We will plan and structure our day in such a way as to reach maximum efficiency without wasting time.

Your dissertation is anywhere from 5,000 – 20,000 words, with the average being 10,000.

In five days a 10,000 word dissertation would work out at 2,000 words per day, does that seem a lot? How many words could you write in a day?

I bet it's more than you think.

Let's start with the **one thing** and our first **FOCUS** from our last chapter.

Don't start with complexity.

This was a big mistake I was making; I'd start with a point in mind, For example:

'People are nicer when they eat chocolate'.

Then I would type it out, slowly thinking of points and going off to shuffle through my sources to find quotes to back it up, rewriting so the paragraphs were perfect, only to find that after a day-long session I had numbered less than 400 words.

Why is it taking me so long!

I was fast at typing. If I had to type the same sentence over and over I'd manage hundreds of pages!

But here's the thing. Thinking on the job is the equivalent of driving a Ferrari down a road that's just twists and speed bumps - it might be fast, but when you have to concentrate on all the obstacles so you'll never be able to open her up.

Sitting there, I realised here I am, desperate for time, floundering with my word count, and yet still I was doing the hardest part of writing (figuring out exactly what needs to go where in a professional, ordered and intellectual manner). In **the most time consuming way possible**, in the middle of the writing itself.

It was like trying to pat my head and rub my stomach at the same time.

I became obsessed with productivity techniques

specifically for writing, researching writers from every genre and walk of life.

(You may not consider yourself a writer, but you have a large portion of writing going on right now, and so you may as well take tips from the best and breeze it!)

I had an epiphany, from none other than Stephen King. (How on earth does he write such a long, high quality novel in just three months?).

Here's what I began to do:

Instead of doing what I was doing, I would open a blank word document, (some writers use an old fashioned pen and paper) and scribble in very short hand an abbreviated version of the chapter or page on paper.

Do this yourself as your first thing. Don't go into any detail, just note what you are looking to write when the time comes. By setting out what you wish to achieve you have no excuse to be stuck, as you constantly can refer to your map, and so no time is wasted leaning back thinking what to write next.

You might notice, I am also starting with chapter one, not the intro or abstract/hypothesis. This is a concept introduced in "Writing for Social Scientists" by Howard Becker, as he puts it: "How can I

introduce it if I haven't written it yet?" This is key
for us as our dissertation may change shape along
the way and will save us a lot of time in editing.

My first chapter, entitled **'exploring knight's
values in a medieval story'** (well not exactly,
slightly more dense, however we will look at how to
make simple sentences sound more academic
shortly) looked something like this:

Chapter One Outline

- Intro, dates, specify when and where these
  stories came from.
- A name for the code 'chivalry', Was it well
  known? Why? Give examples.
- What did it mean to people? Did it mean
  different things? Add social class, Gender.
  Find quotes by ctrl F in the doc, keywords
  'female, male, woman, man, class'.
- What story in particular? Yvian.
- How does the character show these traits?
  Examples
- Cross this with an academic source to back it
  up
- Was it achievable?
- Further depth of specifics of values,
  examples
- How does another character not show these
  traits? Examples

- Deconstruct the 'code of chivalry'
- Confliction in the code, reference Yvain story examples.
- Conclude. Story is silly because modern audience wouldn't accept ending. Examples why? Reference and pull together chapter.

Writing a short outline of your work may take you 20 minutes, but it will save you hours or days of wondering where you should take the next sentence. Write up ultra-fast descriptions. With an outline you can steer the narrative toward where you'd like it to go, rather than snaking all over the topic.

Essentially, if you want to write faster the first step, again, is to **know what you're writing before you write it**. Writing this out in words you actually want other people to read, especially if you're *making everything up as you go along, it takes FOREVER.* It's horribly inefficient and when you get yourself in a dead end, you end up trashing hundreds, sometimes thousands of words to get out. But jotting it down? Takes no time at all. If the part you're sketching out does not flow properly you see it straight away and can change it. That's it. No words lost, **no time wasted.**

Every writing session, dedicate five minutes (sometimes more, never less) and write out a quick description of what you are going to write. It doesn't have to even be a paragraph, but you will be ahead of 80% of the people around you in speed when you get into your chapters. This simple hack can boost your word count enormously. I personally went from writing under 400 words a day to over 2k in a six hour timeslot (with a few breaks, I'm not a madman), and that was taking it really easy.

Let's go back to **Pareto's law,** and incorporate time.

When writers need to boost output, they need to know how much they output in the first place. From personal interviews with article writers to bestselling Novelists, a universal trend seems to be that productivity increases when you are in a place you subconsciously or consciously associate with work. (I.E, not at home!).

It's the same reason people with screens and devices in the bedroom are more likely to be insomniacs, their minds associate the space with thinking and doing, not sleeping.

It's the same with work.

For me, it was the Library. On some occasions at the start of my journey I would have the best intentions of staying in my room and knocking out a great number of words in the comfort of my own home. After all, the library is 25 minutes away, there and back and I've lost 50 minutes of potential writing time travelling right? Wrong. I consistently found that I would write near nothing (100-150 words) while sat at home. Distraction is a killer for production.

The inherent blocks and lack of entertainment on university/college PC's, although annoying when you're trying to catch up on Netflix, is actually a blessing. You are **forced** to be productive in the environment itself. (Do not go with friends unless they are workaholics and will not distract you, be harsh in your judgement, you can make small talk all summer with a first under your belt).

(If you're moving around then utilise storage services like Dropbox, Google drive, or Onedrive. I use Onedrive as it's built into windows 8 onwards).

Timing part 2. Bum time.

Here's a short math test.

Question one: You are now capable of 500 words an hour, on Saturday you spend five hours in the Library, how many words have you written?

Question two: On Sunday, you spend an hour in the Library, how many words have you written?

Answer one: Probably around 3000
Answer two: Probably around 250

It's another common trend that, when writing for longer stints, we are more productive. In the time it takes for you to settle down, get your plan written and write, you are just getting started when the hour rolls around.

It's the same with interruptions. If you turn around every ten minutes to have a chat with your friends, you're going to interrupt your state of mind that we will for examples sake call '*flow*'.

It's true when they say 'go with the flow'! If you have a **specified path**, a **distraction free environment** and a **lengthier period in which to write**, your word count will go through the roof.

Your *flow* can be an individual thing, are you a morning person or a night owl? Me, being the latter, would churn out my best work in the hours of 10pm – 3am. Jake, however, preferred to work from 9am till after lunch.

Bonus Part: Enthusiasm

This is as we discussed in 'finding your question' but relevant here also. It might seem obvious, but this is also **why** we choose a topic that we enjoy to begin with. Writing 15,000 words on the evolution of spoon shape from the 16th century might make things unnecessarily hard for you. Writing 15,000 words on something you've loved since you were a child might make it easier to reach a *flow* state.

CHAPTER 6
WRITING STYLE

"Any intelligent fool can make things bigger, more complex... It takes a touch of genius -- and a lot of courage -- to move in the opposite direction." – Albert Einstein

Okay so productivity is up, you have absorbed the tools for creating hundreds more words per minute. Now, how about style? For example, this book is not designed to be academic, it's designed to be easy to read and absorbed quickly as if talking to a friend.

However, when you're writing your dissertation, things aren't so simple. Examiners are prone to a rather archaic style of writing of the type Mr.Einstein would hate.

Let's take a (finished) example sentence from my dissertation. (Beware! It 'sounds' dense and elaborate but will be explained afterwards!):

The idealised version of the knight the clerics and knights themselves knew to be propaganda could not, in reality, exist. This led unequivocally to the actual knight being fallible in his aim for absolute righteousness.

In terms of work sounding 'academic', not bad, but it didn't start this way.

As suggested earlier, my first paragraph was far from this level of written complexity, and don't worry, so will yours be. As I was concentrating on pushing out my points and sentences as quickly as possible, I did not pause from writing in order to think of a different word for 'kind of', I simply typed 'kind of' and moved on.

Let's take my first sentence in a simpler format:

The kind of knight the clerics and knights themselves knew not to exist made the actual knight flawed in his aim to be sin-free.

I had a point and I made it, very simply, then I kept typing. At the end of each chapter, we will go back and edit it, in order to make it longer and basically, (I know it sounds bad, but it's the truth), harder to read.

What have you done to us, o' educational system, in that we have to purposely replace words in order to make ourselves seem like a walking thesaurus when we clearly are not - you may lament.

Don't fret, we can turn our simple sentences into more drawn out showmanship that markers **like to see** with relative ease. (Yes, I visited several different tutors with two sets of sentences, both making the exact same point, but one changed **solely** with some separate, 'more complex' words, or perhaps just more sparsely used ones. The results were as expected in that every single tutor said they would mark 20% higher if the 'higher' standard of writing was kept up throughout.)

To do with showing a broad and relevant lexicon? Maybe. Simply pretentious? Also, maybe.

All we know for definite is that it is **preferred**, so we'll play the game.

If you are using Microsoft Word or any other highly regarded word processor then you will likely have a thesaurus built in, if not you have, **www.thesaurus.com**.

Thesauruses are **absolutely invaluable** in writing a dissertation at a high grade. If you happen to discuss a dissertation with someone who sounds overly academic in theirs, don't be put off, you can bet your last bit of overdraft that they are using one profusely even when they say they're not.

Here are the exact steps I used to spruce up my sentence:

- I went from 'kind', to 'type', to 'version'. (Simply for variety as I hadn't used 'version' yet.)
- Now instead of: *The kind of knight*

- I had: *The version of knight*

Now what do we do? We describe it more fully! Because we give the tutors what they want!

- I knew that this version of knight was in the simplest of terms, 'good'. (Type in 'good' if you're stuck, you'll be on complex words with one click.) I typed 'ideal' and came across 'idealised'.
- Giving me: *The idealised version of the knight*

This does not take long in editing, and is a hell of a lot faster than making it perfect first time, or god forbid, using your own lexical knowledge to make it perfect first time. (Top tip, if you don't fully understand a word check it in the built in dictionary, sometimes related words aren't the same. Don't use it if you haven't sussed its meaning.)

Now some conventions apply here, namely that as you are writing for academics you will be writing like an academic. If you have spent any time at university you should have, at some point, come across academic work (come on, I imagine I'm safe in assuming that much). The best examples to mirror are those.

CHAPTER 7
STRUCTURING, DRAWING CONCLUSIONS, AND COLLECTING AND USING DATA WHILE WRITING

Fantastic, now we have techniques for productivity and plans for our chapters and pages. Now we have to find a structure for our whole dissertation and the content within it. Luckily, we will use the same structure on the macro and micro scales.

The Rule of Three's

The number three holds a special place in human psychology, we somehow find things in three's very easy to understand and therefore more enjoyable to read. We like enjoyable things and therefore your tutor will like your dissertation! Simple, right?

Simplify into Three's

We start by breaking into the smallest parts, **paragraphs** and **sentences**. We will lay out our paragraphs like this:

1st sentence: A point about your topic. For example, 'Men prefer mustangs'.
2nd sentence: 'Someone says this about it' and (optional) 'someone else says this'

3rd sentence: 'This could possibly mean that/this alludes to'

This will be the format for 80% of your sentences in your dissertation. We have a mark from the point, a mark from the quotes and a mark for you telling the marker that you have **interpreted it in this way**.

Notice I did not say, **a mark for understanding it correctly**. This is very important.

There's no right answer

You could write that **Hitler hated the British**; a source close to him said **he referred to them as 'the hated British bulldogs'**, his childhood friend wrote about a time when he was attacked by a bulldog as a child. This **could possibly** mean that Hitler's entire quest for world domination stemmed from his hate of a certain breed of dog and his subconscious desire to enact revenge from a childhood incident. (If you add in unnecessary sex somewhere you'll do great in Freudian psychology).

Okay yes, that is completely ridiculous and I've just made it up, but really, who's to say it isn't correct? If I could back it up with sources then I've technically just stated a possible explanation based on the information I've been provided with. (To our knowledge Hitler wasn't attacked by a bulldog in his youth, though we're fairly certain he wasn't fond of the British).

Three on a macro scale

Not only will we lay out our **sentences in three's**, we will lay out the **entire dissertation** in this way:

- Intro, or 'what do I expect to find?'
- **Chapter 1: A point**
- **Chapter 2: B point**
- **Chapter 3: A point vs B point**
- Conclusion, or 'did I find what I expected to find?'

This is the primary content of your dissertation. An intro and conclusion yes, but just **three main chapters**. Our other pages such as our bibliography, contents and abstract will be **left to last**. This is not how we are conventionally taught to complete a dissertation, but we are not conventional.

For example, here are the chapter titles of a friend of mine, studying German. They are finished Chapter titles, so don't be intimidated, you'll be there by the end of this book:

- Chapter 1 - The Use and Abuse of English in German Advertising
-To what extent is the use of English in German advertising hindering the comprehension of the

target audience?

- Chapter 2 - <u>The Appropriation of English into the German language</u>

-To what extent is 'Denglisch' contributing to communication barriers in Germany?

- Chapter 3 - <u>The Conservation of a Language</u>

-Is it necessary to protect the German language?

In terms of the A, B, A+B, they are simplified as:

A. How is 'Denglish' being created?
B. How is 'Denglish' affecting the language?
C. Compare A+B and examine if conservation is necessary.

This concluded with the summing up of the discussion in these three chapters and then presenting the findings – but more on conclusions later.

This brings us to an important point on data collection for sentence construction; it goes against most ways essay writing is taught, if you are prepared for the gods of academia to shun while you do little more than a fraction of the work. Read ahead.

Pay as you spend Vs Pre loaded.

Let's say you have to buy electricity for your

university house, if you are still living at home then lucky you, odds are you eat better and your living space is tidier than most students.

Okay, you have three months left in the house and two options.

1. You load the meter with money, in this case you think £100 will be enough for three months.
2. You 'pay as you use', whatever amount you use in three months will be sent to you in order to pay at the end of the period.

You choose option one, because that's how people pay the meter where you are and you decide to follow the crowd. (Just for the sake of example!)

At the end of the month you're packing up your stuff for the summer and you check the electricity meter. – And you have a whole £43.46 left! But wait, you pre-paid and now you can't get the money back! You look out your window with a melancholy sigh, *that could have been jagerbombs..*

The decision is a no brainer here, obviously. When applied to electricity and jagerbombs it's easy to understand wastage is a no-no. We are going to apply the same concept to our quotation collection.

Quotations

Here's an example sentence from my dissertation, talking about the character Kay:

The knight Kay is portrayed as a similar character, and although he does not directly betray Yvain he is seen as rude, immodest and malicious at every point. 'Kay is the anti-hero. He displays all the worthless qualities that a knight may have'.

I wanted to show what Kay stood for, I'd typed out he was a bad guy, but who's to believe me? How did I incorporate a quote into the sentence?

1. I found an academic work using my university library online portal, you will have access to one either through your library or online, every major university is hooked up to one.

2. On the portal there is a search option. In my case I searched for **'Yvian and the knight of the Lion'**, one of my primary sources.

3. I was presented with a list of sources with **'Yvian and the knight of the Lion'** in its title or within the document. I found one that seemed relevant and simply searched the word 'Kay' within it. (Search any document or page using the control and F key together, biggest tip in this book if you don't know it.)

4. I clicked next until I saw one describing Kay, read it once and copied and pasted it in. **I did not** read the entire article, I did not waste time. The sentence was adequate and sounded correct in my work and so I used it.

5. I kept this minimized while I worked, until I had a few sources up and was adding quotes in at random from the different sources. You can use the same source many times, but obviously you need quite a few to make your work look more legitimate and well thought out. Our aim is **not to let the marker know** we completed our dissertation in five days after all!

Let's look at a longer, denser, (and slightly more boring) extract and see if we can get our heads around it:

'Being the 'celebrities' of medieval times any trait possessed by the knight would have been seen as a good standpoint on which to base one's own morals. This idyllic version of knighthood was alongside stories of 'Olympic champions, Bedouin poets and Balkan warriors', all of whom could be considered celebrities.[1] This by proxy would encompass the population of young men and children the story reached who would aspire to be more like their heroes. The Catholic

---

[1] Anderson Kleinberg, 'ARE SAINTS CELEBRITIES?': Some medieval Christian examples', *Cultural and social history*, (2011) v.8 (3) 374-401 (p.393).

Church could easily then latch on to this fame for their own ends. This gives reason for the many illustrations of the time that seem to show the knight and religion as a mixed entity (fig 1).[2] The positives of fame for the church are nicely summed up by Simon Morgan. 'The celebrity is a known individual who has become a marketable commodity. The point at which a public person becomes a celebrity is the point at which a sufficiently large audience is interested in their actions, image and personality to create a viable market for commodities carrying their likeness and for information about their lives and views.' In this Clerical writers could validate their blessing of knighthood in an openly pragmatic manner. For of course, in the eyes of the church, the chivalric knight was needed to protect clerical property, defend the homeland and suppress or hang heretics. These rationalisations were considered by some a ruse that simply 'eased the clerical path to sanctified violence'.[3]

Let's look into this more deeply as, to a marker, my extract seems well thought out and educated.

Firstly, I have followed the three point paragraph, essentially:

1. The church wanted in on the knight's fame.
2. Quote explaining why knight's image was valuable, reference to picture showing religion and knighthood mixed.
3. Some people think/This could possibly

---

[2] *Holy Warriors : The Religious Ideology of Chivalry.* Cover.
[3] *Holy Warriors : The Religious Ideology of Chivalry.* P. 68.

mean that - the church were using knighthood to sanctify violence.

Broken down, the point is simple, and cannot easily be argued with. After all you are not taking a side, and you are not basing this on opinion but simply information you have been presented with.

How did it get so refined? I must have done a lot of reading on the subject to come to these conclusions, right?

Wrong.

I typed the entirety of my points out in huge sittings of many words and then **added the quotes in after**. It didn't even matter what the quotes were because, really, I was just adding them to sound more academic.

Here's a tip, **you can add quotes out of context if they sound good.** You have to have a point, for example I wanted to explain that knights were famous. So I basically typed, 'knights were very famous', in a drawn out manner, used my thesaurus a lot, and then when I went back to add my quotes I skimmed until I saw a line that said 'Olympic champions, Bedouin poets and Balkan warriors' and incorporated it into my own work.

It's not even cheating, it's just doing things

differently. I was aiming for a good grade, nothing else. I achieved it, and so can you.

In traditional teaching, we would read on our topic, find out a fact and decide to use it **by** quoting the author. We explain what we have found and compare other quotes. Essentially, I advocate the opposite.

Adding quotations is a fantastic opportunity to save our references in order to easily complete our footnotes and bibliography. It saves us searching for the same article again and wasting time. There are easy tools to do this included in the chapter 'Reference and Bibliography cheat-sheet'.

A quick note on Dissertation Logs

Many dissertations nowadays include a 'dissertation log', a weekly log of what activities you undertook and the reading you did. This in some cases is worth up to 15%, in some it is only worth 5%. You should use the techniques outlined here to fill it in retrospectively at the end and save you more time. A common format for a dissertation log is a weekly diary of actions completed, for example: Jan week 1, Jan week 2, Jan week 3, Etc.

As you may be completing this in five days, there is obviously no way to go back in time to fill this out properly. You should fill it out in a believable way, taking certain sources you pick up while writing your chapters and adding them at certain dates. A good way to add credibility and mass to your log is to look up (very quickly) a few sources around the topic and include them in for example 'January week 3', then in 'March week 2', include that you took these sources out as they either weren't relevant enough or you decided to approach the topic from a different angle.

CHAPTER 8
INTRODUCTION, ABSTRACT AND CONCLUSION

Arrr matey, here be Three's

The number three is back. This time we're taking it to the big leagues.

So, our dissertation chapters are now set out in three, Chapter A, Chapter B and Chapter B&C.

Further to that, we will say that our dissertation is like a fancy dinner. (When was the last time anyone completing a dissertation while neck deep in overdraft had a fancy dinner? Alas.)

Our dissertation has a prelude, or starter, a main course, and dessert, or conclusion. It's sweet because it's the last hurdle!

Okay three parts, simple.

Part One: Abstract and Introduction
Part Two: Chapters with discussion
Part Three: Conclusion with references

Your abstract

After your title page, even before your contents, comes your Abstract. It is a complete summary of your dissertation, usually no more than 250 words long. (This may be called 'résumé' or simply 'summary' depending on where you are.

Usually your abstract would be important as it serves as a means to let readers know what they're in for before deciding if they want to commit to actually reading your work. As your dissertation tutor is forced to read the entirety of your dissertation anyway and will probably be the only one who ever does, this is rather ironic. (Aside, obviously, from the parents and friends you will try to force it on because you worked bloody hard on it and god damn it someone else better read it aside from that old guy who doesn't care anyway.)

Anyway, your abstract, being an overview of your whole study. Your research question, discussion and results, can't be written until you've pretty much finished your dissertation anyway. Which for us is very soon.

Introduction

After you've let your tutor know what they're in for, and, surprise surprise, they're going to read it, you will be prepping them more in depth about your question and chosen topic.

An introduction can be anywhere from 1-4 pages long, with the average at 2. Some simple tips for your introduction are as follows:

- You're looking to inspire an interest in your work, (or try too!)
- You're looking to explain something about the background.
- You should give reasons for choosing your dissertation topic.

Follow these quick fire questions that will help you write the introduction quickly and efficiently.

- What inspired you to study this particular topic and why?
- Explain it's background
- What are your main sources?
- What do you expect to find and why?
- How? Are you exploring a theoretical argument or collecting data?
- How will you set this out?
- Bonus: Is it important to the particular field of study? If so why? – this isn't necessary but include if you can or feel like it.

Conclusion

Pow, it's time for dessert, and we're not full.

We can finally start to be less abstract here. We discussed a particular topic in a particular area of study for three chapters and we found out some important things, we interpreted them in a certain way, life lessons were learned.

What do we really need to let the marker know? Let's have a look at our cheat sheet:

- A (minor) summary of our three main chapters
- Your deductions, based on those chapters, did you find what you expected? If so or if not, why?
- A personal opinion on the discussion
- The implications of your work. Will it be useful for further study?
- What limited your work? If you were to write this again knowing what you know now, what would you do differently? How could you further your research?

This will be the end of your work, tie it all up neatly by following the cheat sheet and then editing it afterward to make it academic. Remember to consider all your findings and accentuate **what you deducted from them** succinctly.

Reiterate, what were you aiming to find? You targeted specific areas of research; did they reinforce what you originally thought?

Don't forget your research question! Write a

helpful sentence at the top of the page with your title question if you need to, I included a brief intro in mine, below:

'From the outset, the aim of this dissertation was to determine whether medieval fantasy fiction of the era of the middle ages was more or less representative of the culture of knights than its same genre contemporary counterpart. This chapter will collaborate the findings on the subject.'

This not only helped the marker follow along, it helped me in writing it as I could keep on track of the aim of my conclusion as I wrote and helped me to be memorable and succinct. The facts we collect from our work we will infer using a logical approach of the Aristotelian variety, namely.

All A's are B's
C is an A
Therefore C is a B

(Even Aristotle liked three's).

We cannot be wrong is we use this logic for facts, no assumptions will be made without data and it will stop us from making wild deductions without evidence.

A little more on logic

We can also use this inversely, so with words an

example could be:

No woman is a King
Helen is a woman
Therefore she is not a King

However, when drawing deductions from your work, don't fall into what is known as **logical fallacy** (false logic). This is characterised as:

No woman is a King
Dave is not a woman
Therefore Dave is a King

This happens when you forget that you have not specified that everything that *isn't* a woman *is* a King.

Keep to those rules and your logic will be unwavering, absolute and leave your marker with no choice but to pour marks all over your work!

Using Logic to show that you couldn't use logi- wait what.

So, you don't have the data to come to one of the conclusions you'd have liked to. Be sure to **include it**. This, 'showing off the limitations' of your work proves you're **aware of the limitations**, putting in this as an extra will rack up some extra marks without even having **to do** anything but **explain what you couldn't do**!

CHAPTER 9
BIBLIOGRAPHY, FOOTNOTES AND REFERENCING CHEAT SHEET.

It is after three years of university lectures, essay writing and further study that some of us realise, when adding to our dissertation, that we can't actually reference properly.

In the UK, ironically we most commonly use the 'Harvard Referencing System', which begs a particular layout for both footnotes and bibliography references.

However, we can save ourselves a ton of time learning and implementing this by having a tool to pretty much do all the work for us!

There are many of these, one I personally have had luck with is www.citethisforme.com, it's well known among students who want to get their bibliography right first time and do it quicker than anyone else. (Also, I have no affiliation with any websites mentioned in this book. These particular sites have simply helped me in the past and I feel obliged to pass them on. A simple Google search however will bring up many alternatives!)

We will start with our bibliography. Bring up the site and do as follows:

1. Add your sources.

Fill in the details you know from each source you've used in your essay or assignment

2. Choose your style.

For us, this is most probably Harvard. However if not, there are many others to choose from.

3. Copy and Paste, or download the bibliography in Word format. Done!

'Cheating' makes referencing fun! (Well, almost.) Here's a picture of the page as it looked August 2015.

Bibliography, sorted. I'm not going into any further detail with this because I don't advocate typing out the references yourself when you can get your hands on perfectly useful tools this easily. If you come across someone who thinks it's immoral, then they were probably the type of fellow to have a go at people who looked up words when the dictionary was invented, because *it's right to do things in the longest fashion possible you know!*

Anyway, for referencing on actual pages with footnote, you can't beat 'The Queen's University Belfast referencing tool', this is an amazing time saver, at:

www.qub.ac.uk/cite2write/harvard31.html

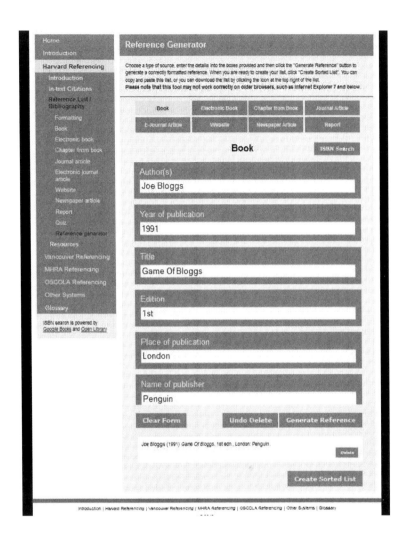

The generator will look something like this, here's another screenshot from the year of publishing, 2015.

It's criminally easy to use, just do the following:

Enter your information, editions, year published, etc.

'Generate Reference'

Either copy and paste the finished reference or, if you have many, keep generating them and click 'create sorted list'.

Footnotes, in case you don't know, go at the bottom of your page and link at the end of your sentence. **Not in the middle of it.** Always at the full stop or other punctuation marking the end of the sentence. This is an **easy mistake to make** and translates to marks wasted for no reason! (Take a look at the sample dissertation for ideas on layout.

CHAPTER 10
POLISHING THE FINAL PRODUCT
AND PRESENTATION

Here you have it, perhaps not held in your hands, but at least metaphorically so. Your dissertation 1.0, a complete set of files!

Let's make it look groovy.

This applies to grammar, punctuation and title layout just as much as your font and front page!

Here's a great tip, if you can, one to two days before your deadline arrange a meeting with your tutor for them to give what you've got a look over. You should have enough material by then for this to prove useful, although they will not want to read your whole dissertation there and then. (If they can and they give notes you're in real luck.) Personally I brought what I considered my 'best page' for them to read, and three I thought could be my worst pages. I went through all three bad pages and got great direct changes that helped me make subtle changes to some of my other work. Then I showed my best page for moral and to get confirmation on what I was doing right. Remember, **small wins keep up morale**!

As for spelling and grammar, you **cannot** forget

to use spellcheck, a real schoolboy if you don't, however most of us students have been using it since school so not a big mention. (Hint, in word 2010+ it's under the 'review' tab.)

Typeface is a commonly customised aspect, below are my recommended font for a mix of readability and professionalism.

Arial*
Century
Courier New*
Garamond
Georgia*
Lucida Bright
Microsoft Sans Serif
Tahoma – (the bolds can look funny after printing.)
Times New Roman*
Trebuchet MS*
Verdana*

Size should be 11pt – 14pt, the latter being more commonly used if struggling with word count, which after chapter six, we shouldn't be!

Often, your university will ask you to leave a line blank every other line, (see example dissertation at the end.) this can be done in word 2010+ under the 'page layout' tab.

Here's a hard part, with all this quick writing, there still may be sentences or parts of your work may have to be changed or **abandoned altogether**. Don't fear the reaper! We're including more complex sentences to make us sound academic, however if a sentence provides no value or insight whatsoever it's simply filler and should really be abandoned, no matter how intelligent it sounds. Have too many of these sentences and your marker will start to get suspicious. Suspicious markers are tricky markers so let's keep them with the idea that we're straight laced intellectuals that don't take shortcuts. (In other words, fools!).

Revising and proofreading

Revisions of your work are key, but with a 5 day timeframe it's hard to get someone to proofread the entire thing before you hand it in. This is where I recommended finding a dissertation buddy to **swap with**.

Now when you have your head in the game with just one day to deadline and you're steaming through on schedule, the last thing you want to do is abandon your work for even 30 minutes to read someone else's. I cannot stress enough that if you can, **Do it.**

I'll cover this even if you aren't one of these people, but just in case. – Some people are funny about this. Don't be one of those guys that are so protective of their work they become secretive in case someone 'steals their ideas', this isn't **Microsoft vs. Apple.** This will only **provide value** to you **both.**

You read through theirs, they read through yours. With a fresh pair of eyes mistakes are glaringly obvious, you may even pick up some phrase or style that you want to quickly edit in, the person reading yours might do the same. **Great**, you have improved **your** dissertation quickly and easily, and your mate/random library dude's as well! It's **win win.** Paying for a proofreading service is wasted time and money when you've got willing proof-readers next to you already.

Checking yourself

If you're really stuck, you can check your words individually yourself by reading backwards. It bypasses your mind trying to read for meaning and makes mistakes easier to spot. If you're checking for flow, or ease of readability, try reading it out loud. (Perhaps not in the library).

CHAPTER 11
A FULL EXAMPLE DISSERTATION

One of the biggest problems students face when attempting to write their dissertations is having no reference point. How can you be expected to write something in a form you've never seen?

Below is a full dissertation, to the grade of 2:1, in the subject English Literature. It has not been 'tarted up' in any form and is as it was the day it was handed in. This is done on **purpose** as there are quite a few schoolboy errors in it such as typos, sentences that don't really make sense and other minor but obvious wrongdoings. Let these mistakes bolster you, as this was still marked at a high 2:1. With proper care following the procedures in this book, you won't make the same mistakes and will be well on your way to a 1ˢᵗ class. (I certainly wouldn't have made them had I perfected some of the latter techniques like proof-reading!)

An Analysis on the Presentation of the Knight's Code of Chivalry In Medieval Fantasy Fiction.

Abstract

This dissertation explores the concept of the Knight's code of chivalry as presented in European medieval fantasy fiction. Specifically I will investigate Arthurian legend and in particular provide an examination of Chretien De troyes' *Yvain: The Knight of The Lion*. I will juxtapose this with a contemporary take on medieval fantasy fiction in the form of George R.R Martin's saga, *A Song of Ice and Fire*.

As a recent work, Martin's *Song of Ice and Fire* has so far left scholarly circles quite unaffected when compared to other titles in the genre. As well as this, the concept of the moral ambiguity in the chivalric code in comparison to Arthurian legend is an entirely neglected one.

The first chapter will explore the presentation of the knight's code of chivalry in Yvain, and will look at its relevance to a medieval audience. In the second chapter I will focus on the representation of the same themes in *A Song of Ice and Fire* and compare them with *Yvain: The Knight of The Lion*. My third chapter will focus on how restrictive conventions of the medieval period may have led to some work being charged with societal, religious or political agendas, and will examine if those same agendas are present in contemporary text. Finally, I will consider if retrospectively, modern writers' tales expose a more reliable representation of medieval culture than the texts that were actually produced in the era.

Contents

Introduction

The word chivalry in the medieval period did not carry the same meaning it does in the contemporary environment, in fact, according to *The Oxford Companion To French Literature*, 'its precise meaning remains elusive: chivalry, as it evolved from the 11th c., meant different things at different times in different places'.[4] In my study I will be looking at the word from the standpoint of the 'knight's code of chivalry', perhaps the most famous of its designations.

The connotation that even the word chivalry conjures in the minds of present-day readers seems to resound with a medieval tone and lexically has largely fallen out of use. When looked at in terms of the medieval literary canon, though, it can be considered a cornerstone of societal normality in certain social class groups, this study will look at how and why this was the case.

Originally, the word chivalry came to be as an offshoot of the archaic French word for 'Knight', spelt 'Chevalier'. This word comes from the Latin 'Caballus' meaning 'Horse'. As the horse was the defining power in medieval times it gives a connotation of importance to the 'Chevaliers' and in turn 'Chivalry'. Richard Barber in *The Reign of Chivalry*, though, assures us that 'the time and place from which medieval knighthood emerged is very different: not the declining years of the roman empire, but the declining years of its successor, the empire of Charlemange'.[5] The reign of Charlemagne and his role on the definition of chivalry was profound in its

---

[4] Patrick Harvey, & Joan Heseltine, *The Oxford companion to French literature*, (Oxford: Clarendon Press, 1959).
[5] Richard .W Barber, *The reign of chivalry*. (New York: St. Martin's Press, 1980). P 85.

spawn of one of my primary texts, *The Song of Roland*.

It could be deducted, then, that a Chivalrous man is powerful and capable of defending himself and others. In contemporary literature however the meaning of Chivalry has shifted to neglect the marital aspects of the code and is often used to describe the more gentlemanly characteristics of a character.

This code of battle in medieval epic fantasy literature is deeply engrained, in terms of the romances we are looking at, Barber argues that 'the magic spell that transmutes mere knighthood into chivalry is that of courtly love'.[6] Of course, this may or may not be true, this essay then will explore the use of courtly love in archaic and contemporary work and look at its effect on the idea of the code of chivalry.

Yvain: The Knight of The Lion is believed to have been written in the 1170's alongside *Lancelot: the knight of the cart*, also by De Troyes, and so is a perfect example of a medieval Arthurian text. Many versions have been written since, but for the purposes of defining the Knight's code of chivalry in the height of the medieval period these romances will be looked at in the eldest form in which they exist.

Martin's 7 book saga is so recent that at the time of writing there are still two books left to be written before the saga is complete, therefore, I will be studying the first five of these books and treating them as a whole. These books as standalone novels are *A Game of Thrones*, *A Clash of Kings*, *A Storm of Swords*, *A Feast for Crows* and *A Dance With Dragons*. The sheer volume of material in these first five books is enough to give tremendous insight into the world of contemporary medieval fantasy fiction and offer a unique view on how the chivalrous knight is presented when

---

[6] *The Reign of Chivalry*. P.55.

recreated today.

A great many medieval fantasy fiction works are accepting of the chivalric code of the knight without question. This leads to most work on the actions of the Medieval knight being drawn with regards to the persona of a character, often labelling them as inherently good or evil. However, *A Song of Ice and Fire* is one with a great sensitivity to the moral ambiguity inherent in the chivalric code. In combination with *Yvain: The Knight of the Lion* it helps bring forward a distinctive line of argument concerning Yvain's actions from the perspective of the pressures of the code of chivalry rather than from Yvain's nature as a character.

As well as this, I will concentrate on certain societal, religious and political pressures of the medieval period and attempt to measure their effect on how the knight's code of chivalry was presented in medieval fantasy fiction. I will also determine if such pressures are in the process of affecting how contemporary medieval fantasy fiction is portrayed.

Chapter One
Exploring the Presentation of the Knight's Code of
Chivalry in *Yvain: The Knight of The Lion.*

Medieval fantasy Literature from the 8th to 15th centuries
saw extensive employment of the concept of the Knight's
code of chivalry. Within this is contained Arthurian legend as
well as the French form of epic poetry *chaston de geste.*[7] In the
case of this chapter both will be investigated.

The knight's code of chivalry was widely known among
the medieval audience since its inception. This can be
associated with *The Song of Roland*, an example of the epic
chaston de geste genre.[89]. As a code of knightly virtue it was
hugely publicised in the ballads, poems and stories spread by
travelling bards and minstrels of the era as well as its'
literature. Arthurian legend stands at the forefront of the
contemporary readers knowledge of the period. King Arthur
and the Knights of the Round Table the face of the well-
known legends of the time. In particular these stories have
survived to be told more frequently than others from the era,
perhaps because of their epic nature. In the story of *Yvain*
specifically the knight's code of chivalry is presented
throughout as integral to every action of a knight, Chretien
describing them as 'those goodly chosen knights who spent
themselves for honour's sake'.[10] Honour being in keeping as
one of the sworn oaths of knighthood.

There are mixed opinions on what chivalry meant to
Yvain. McConnell believes that 'chivalry, for Yvain, was a

[7] Crosland, *The Old French Epic*, (New York: Haskell House, 1951). P.36
[8] Dorothy. L Sayers, *The Song of Roland*, (Harmondsworth: Penguin Books, 1957).
[9] Chrétien De Troyes & Burton Raffel. *Yvain:, the Knight of the Lion*, (New Haven: Yale University Press, 1987).
[10] *Yvain: the Knight of the Lion.* P.3

matter of social class' as he without a second guess names the wild herdsman 'herran', an old English term for minstrel or peasant upon his first meeting.[11] The relevance of social class in the chivalric code is summarised in short according to William W. Comfort:

> '*As an ideal of social conduct, the code of chivalry never touched the middle and lower classes, but it was the religion of the aristocracy and of the twelfth-century "honnete homme". Never was literature in any age closer to the ideals of a social class. So true is this that it is difficult to determine whether social practices called forth the literature, or whether, as in the case of the seventeenth-century pastoral romance in France, it is truer to say that literature suggested to society its ideals.*'[12]

This 'Herran' asks Yvain to tell him 'what kind of a man thou art, and what thou seekest here'. It is a credit to the celebrity of knighthood that a man who would claim to be a knight is expected to be true of the code of chivalry, Yvain proves this is in his reply. `I am, as thou seest, a knight seeking for what I cannot find; long have I sought without success'.[13] Essentially, Yvain's reply to the question of what kind of man he is could be construed as simply, 'as you can see, I am knight'. The reply seems to need no elaboration, perhaps due to the connotations the title of knight holds. The code's portrayal in the story is essentially what makes a knight. Of course, as a middle class social group, the knight may only considered along with perhaps his physical assets such as armour and his horse. It is in Calgorant's story, for example, where he claims he 'was making way in search of

---

[11] Winder McConnell, 'The Dream of Chivalry: A Study of Chrétien De Troyes's Yvain and Hartmann von Aue's Iwein', MLN. 100, 3 (1985), 686-688 (p.687)
[12] Legends of Camelot (2000) *Chretien De Troyes' Arthurian Romances*. [online] Available at: http://gorddcymru.org/twilight/camelot/chretien/wwcomfort_intro.htm [Accessed: 11 Apr 2013].
[13] *Yvain: the Knight of the Lion,* P.67.

adventures, fully armed as a knight should be'.[14]

It also is clear that Yvain is fearsomely proud of his vows and his honour, so much so that at the point of the story where Yvain realises he has broken his word, it is obvious the news wounds him deeply. He would 'rather be banished alone in some wild land, where no one would know where to seek for him, and where no man or woman would know of his whereabouts', as, 'he hates nothing so much as he hates himself, nor does he know to whom to go for comfort in the death he has brought upon himself. But he would rather go insane than not take vengeance upon himself, deprived, as he is, of joy through his own fault.'[15] Chrétien creates a rather elaborate image of penance that is especially prominent in that Yvain feels the need to 'take vengeance' upon himself as opposed to being punished by another. The deeply rooted religious ideology of penance for sins among knights is similar to the issues raised by Richard Kaeuper in *Holy Warriors : The Religious Ideology of Chivalry* in which Kaeuper introduces 'a graded scale of penance' according to the severity of the sin.[16] As traditionally the clerics were responsible for carrying out penance on the sins of knights ('Whether or not these penances were effectively carried out is unclear, but the direction of thought is significant') it surely took courage for a knight to own up and confess his sins.[17] Yvain here is portrayed in this instance as the ideal knight, for he would rather face madness than not take penance on himself for the vow he has broken.

That said, some would declare the chivalric code

---

[14] *Yvain: the Knight of the Lion,* P.11.

[15] *Yvain: the Knight of the Lion,* P.121.

[16] Richard W Kaeuper, *Holy Warriors : The Religious Ideology of Chivalry,* University of Pennsylvania Press. (2012) <http://lib.myilibrary.com?ID=421089> [accessed 28 March 2013] (P.168).

[17] *Holy Warriors : The Religious Ideology of Chivalry.* P 168

demanded of a knight the near impossible. The expectations of the code required the equilibrium between Christian faith, skill at arms, heroics and courtly love. All of which were balancing precariously between the knights moral and social persona, the slightest decision being hugely impactful. A knight was as good as his reputation according to Gawain, but to tell of too many past victories may find the knight guilty of the sin of pride. When thinking of his sins Yvain exclaims, 'may God defend me from ever giving place to such pride as to let them fall at my feet!' Too few victories and they would garner little respect and be considered a coward. A moral struggle is outlined many times throughout the story to accentuate how the knight tries to be in keeping with his vows no matter what injuries or hardships he has to overcome. Yvain in De Troyes story is summarised by Kratin as 'a perfect knight from the start' and that 'contrary to modern expectations of fictional characterizations, Yvain does not develop.'[18] It certainly seems from the story that Yvain is encompassing of the knightly virtues in some respects. It cannot be ignored, though, that the entire story is set around the breaking of his oath to Laudine.

In relation to the Knight's code of chivalry, though, the vows Yvain swore to his life partner may have been contradictory to what was expected of him as a knight. To determine this, we must first narrow down the exact nature and specifics of the code, beginning with *The song of Roland*.

The Song of Roland is a great example of a work that is one of the first to encompass the Knights code of chivalry in the times of Arthurian legend. The work describes 8th century knights and the battles Emperor Charlemagne fought in the Dark Ages. It has since been described as 'Charlemagne's code of chivalry', with *The song of Roland* becoming the most famous *chanson de geste*, or 'song of heroic deeds' hugely

---

[18] Ojars Kratins, 'Love and Marriage in Three Versions of "The Knight of the Lion"', *Comparative Literature*, 16 (1964), 31-41 (p.38)

popular from 1000ad to 1500ad.[19] The author of *The Song of Roland* is uncertain, it may have been written by a French poet known as Turold between 1140 and 1170, although it seems most of the alterations of the work were completed up until 1198.[20] Some argue the poem was written even earlier, as it gives credit to the theory that it was inspired by the Castilian campaigns of the 1030s and therefore would have been a major influence of the first crusade, which will enter discussion further on.

The work itself describes the death of Count Roland in an epic battle in the Pyranee Mountains against the Saracens after he is betrayed by his former ally Ganelon. In *The Reign of Chivalry* by Richard barber the similar stylistic points of The Song of Roland are commented on.

Loyalty, comradeship and prowess are the knight's great virtues: their counterparts are treachery, faithlessness and cowardice, and just as Roland is perfect, so nothing good can be said of the traitor Ganelon. Even his noble birth seems a kind of reproach, making his abasement all the more acute. It is a black and white world of absolutes, powerfully described.[21]

The Anti-hero Ganelon is described as the absolute opposite of the embodiment of the code, if better to show the good virtues of Roland beside him. In Yvain, the knight Kay is portrayed as a similar character, and although he does not directly betray Yvain he is seen as rude, immodest and malicious at every point. 'Kay is the anti-hero. He displays all the worthless qualities that a knight may have. Chrétien uses him more as a display piece than as a real character - here is the sort of knight that one should not aim to emulate.'[22]

---

[19] Geneviève Hasenohr and Michel Zink, 'Dictionnaire des lettres françaises: Le Moyen Age' in *La Pochothèque* (Paris: Fayard, 1992)

[20] Ian Short, "Introduction", *La Chanson de Roland*, (France: Le Livre de Poche, 1990), p. 13.

[21] Richard .W Barber, *The reign of chivalry*. (New York: St. Martin's Press, 1980). P 85.

[22] *The reign of chivalry*, P.85.

Although not a knight that one would seek to imitate, Kay at no point commits any truly atrocious acts. If read today, Kay simply comes across as an irritable and unnecessarily provocative knight. The furthest anyone gets to reprimanding him is when the queen tells him, 'you are troublesome and mean thus to annoy your companions.'[23] After which he they almost completely ignore the knight, reassuring that Kay 'is so accustomed to evil speech that one cannot punish him for it.'[24]

The Song of Roland outlines seventeen virtues of the Knights code of chivalry, they are as follows:

- To fear God and maintain His Church
- To serve the liege lord in valour and faith
- To seek out and protect the weak and defenceless
- To give succour to widows and orphans
- To refrain from the wanton giving of offence
- To live by honour and for glory
- To despise pecuniary reward
- To fight for the welfare of all
- To obey those placed in authority
- To guard the honour of fellow knights
- To eschew unfairness, meanness and deceit
- To keep faith
- At all times to speak the truth
- To persevere to the end in any enterprise begun
- To respect the honour of women
- Never to refuse a challenge from an equal
- Never to turn the back upon a foe

Out of these seventeen virtues of the knights code of chivalry only 5 relate to combat according to the *Song of*

Roland, the others are acts of a chivalrous nature.[25] *Medieval Times* describes it as 'a moral system which went beyond rules of combat and introduced the qualities idealized by knighthood, such as bravery, courtesy, honour, and gallantry toward women'.[26]

Aside from not returning to Laudine, which is debatably not part of his knightly vows, Yvain is seen to adhere to these strictly. At one point De Troyes makes the point to quote a virtue almost word for word when Laudine is in need of aid. In an obliviously hypocritical way she unbeknownst turns to the fabled knight of the lion, 'she left the court resolving to devote her life to the search through all the land for the Knight with the Lion, who devotes himself to succouring women in need of aid'.[27]

To examine each virtue that Yvain was expected to follow brings forth questions on the seemingly contradictory nature of the code, as upon inspection, we can see that the interpretation could be seen in more than a few instances as ambiguous. For example, if Yvain were spend his time 'seek[ing] out and protect[ing] the weak and defenceless', it would leave little room for him to also be stationed at his homestead with his new wife. This in turn could in some way cause the breaking of the virtues of living 'by honour' and 'to respect the honour of women'. De Troyes allows us to see in his story how Yvain falls prey to the conflicting vows of marriage and knighthood at the instance in the story where YVAIN is told a husbands duty is to earn glory for his household:

'Now ought your fame to be increased! Slip off the bridle and halter and come to the tournament with me, that no one may say that you are

---

[25] *The song of Roland*, P. 24.

[26] Jane Brown, 'Chivalry' (2011)
<http://medievaltimes.edublogs.org/chivalry/> [Accessed: 25 Mar 2013].

[27] *Yvain: the Knight of the Lion*, P.171.

jealous. Now you must no longer hesitate to frequent the lists, to share in the onslaught, and to contend with force, whatever effort it may cost.[28]

Again we can see the confliction of two vows Yvain has sworn, on the one hand he has his wife, and on the other his brothers in arms who persuade him to live a life befitting a knight and not just a loyal husband. Gawain argues that if Yvain does not come to the tournament him he will be considered 'one of those… who degenerate after marriage'.[29] In essence Gawain's argument is that the knight's duty is to keep the reputation of his name as great warrior so that his household may not fall into disgrace. Ironically, Yvain's friend Gawain seems to be adhering to the chivalric code in earnest, he believes Yvain's duty is to earn glory for his household, and by advising him in this he is seeking to 'guard the honour of [a] fellow knight'. He explains his reasoning to Yvain in such a way that he does not refuse:

'It is not right that affection should be bestowed on him after his worth and reputation are gone. Surely you, too, would have cause to regret her love if you grew soft, for a woman quickly withdraws her love, and rightly so, and despises him who degenerates in any way when he has become lord of the realm.'[30]

It is clear Gawain's argument is that by not partaking in knightly duties he is doing his lady more of a disservice than not being at home with her by bringing his house into disrepute, even going as far as to say if he does not come his lady will grow to resent him anyway.

This original code of chivalry was to go through a constant revision from its inception, changes that would refine it into a simpler set of virtues. Many outside pressures had influence on these subtle changes, which will be looked at in further detail in chapter three. The biggest change to the code though, and one that can be noted here, is the revision by the Duke of Burgundy, in which he would divide it into twelve

---

[28] *Yvain: the Knight of the Lion,* P.130.
[29] *Yvain: the Knight of the Lion,* P.131.
[30] *Yvain: the Knight of the Lion,* P.131.

virtues. These became Faith, Charity, Justice, Sagacity, Prudence, Temperance, Resolution, Truth, Liberality, Diligence, Hope and Valour.[31] Although essentially these meanings were the same as Rolands', it was a significant enough change to spur a reincarnation of the chivalric romance, that most present day works of medieval fantasy fiction will no doubt have been influenced by.

Yvain at the end of De Troyes tale declares, 'I now admit my guilt and sin. I have been bold, indeed, in daring to present myself to you'.[32] This admission of guilt directly contradicts many held notions of Yvain as the ideal knight put forward by Kratin and Eleazer as it directly contradicts the virtue of 'Truth' that is a cornerstone of knightly etiquette[3334] It could be said that the expectation of De Troyes to believe that the reader will have faith in Yvain to be loyal to his renewed vows is somewhat of paradox. Yvain is expected to search for no more adventure or glory, even though he is still a knight and therefore should adhere to the code of chivalry, De Troyes leaves the story with the assumption that Yvain is to stay with Laudine happily ever after. 'He is redeemed and makes an ending… of all the sorrows that he had'.[35] Yvain then goes on the tell Laudine, 'if you will deign to keep me now, I never again shall do you any wrong'.[36] This change in direction for Yvain is badly founded, as the entire story lays the groundwork for Yvain's persona that has in effect repeatedly broken the oaths he has sworn.

[31] Johan Huizinga, *The waning of the middle ages, a study of the forms of life, thought and art in France and the Netherlands in the XIVth and XVth centuries.* (London: E. Arnold & Co, 1924).
[32] *Yvain: the Knight of the Lion.* P.206
[33] 'Love and Marriage in Three Versions of "The Knight of the Lion"'
[34] Roger Hedburg, 'Courtly Love in French Aurthurian Twelfth Century Romances'. <http://voices.yahoo.com/courtly-love-french-aurthurian-twelfth-century-43660.html> [Accessed: 14 Apr 2013].
[35] *Yvain: the Knight of the Lion,* P.210.
[36] *Yvain: the Knight of the Lion,* P.206.

In fact, De Troyes's own assumption in relevance to Yvain's story, wherein he assures that 'lovers used to deserve to be considered courteous, brave, generous, and honourable' is shown at least in Yvain's case to be scarcely true at all, or at least only when it suits him.[37] From *Yvain's* popularity it could be deducted that the medieval audience seemed to be more easily prepared to accept the narrators word, even when the story laid the footwork for an ending that could be argued to be completely contradictory.

---

[37] *Yvain: the Knight of the Lion.* P.6

Chapter Two
Exploring the Presentation of the Knight's Code of Chivalry in *A Song of Ice and Fire* in Comparison to *Yvain: The Knight of The Lion.*

The crisis in *Yvain: The Knight of the Lion* is the breaking of the knight's sworn vows with a literal insanity portrayed by Yvain on his realisation.[38] In Juxtaposition, I will be focusing on George .R.R Martin's saga *A Song of Ice and Fire* and especially the character of Jamie Lannister and his attitude to the knight's code of chivalry.[39]

Martin presents a view of knighthood from Jaime's perspective completely unlike Yvain's. When Jaime is accused of breaking his vows, rather than be turned insane by the prospect, he is indifferent.

'So many vows. They make you swear and swear. Defend the King, obey the King, obey your father, protect the innocent, defend the weak. But what if your father despises the King? What if the King massacres the innocent? It's too much. No matter what you do, you're forsaking one vow or another'.[40]

Jaime's point is a good one, and a view that a real life Yvain may have taken up himself. A medieval reader may, however, have qualms with his nonchalance. The argument could also be founded that that the medieval audience were not subjected to such colossal moral decisions as the characters in Martin's contemporary saga are. For example Linda Antonsson and Elio Garcia describe Jaime as a classic

---

[38] Chrétien De Troyes & Burton Raffel. *Yvain:, The Knight of the Lion*, (New Haven: Yale University Press, 1987).
[39] George R.R Martin, *A Game of Thrones*, (New York, Bantam Books, 1996)
[40] George R.R Martin, *A Clash of Kings*, (New York, Bantam Books, 1996)

example of a Byronic hero.

Named for the great romantic poet Lord Byron , whose characters often exemplified the type, the Byronic hero is "mad, bad, and dangerous to know," and there's a checklist of traits that they often share: cynicism, cunning, disrespect for authority, brilliance, self-destructive behaviour, a troubled past, and so on.[41]

It could be said to be paradoxical to describe a medieval character as a Byronic hero, especially a supposedly chivalric knight, yet in Jaime's case it is entirely appropriate.

No knight in martin's series is completely untainted and held in divine standing though. In the story we are constantly aware that these knights are first and foremost men like everyone else. 'In Westeros, as in the real world, there are few if any saints, or even adults, who do not sin at one level of severity or another.'[42]

If one were to be said to be most in keeping with his vows during the series, one would find it hard to do better than Ser Barristan Selmy. A man of 60, he still has considerable fighting prowess along with a distinguished sense of chivalry, even in the face of foes of a much lower social class.

"Only cowards dress in iron," Khrazz declared, circling. No one wore armor in the fighting pits… Ser Barristan turned with him. "This coward is about to kill you, ser." The man was no knight, but his courage had earned him that much courtesy.[43]

---

[41] James Lowder, *Beyond the Wall: Exploring George R. R. Martin's A Song of Ice and Fire, From A Game of Thrones to A Dance with Dragons.* (Dallas: BenBella Books, 2012), p.9.
[42] *Beyond the Wall,* P. 92.
[43] George R.R Martin, *A Dance with Dragons*, (New York, Bantam Books, 1996), P.154

Chretien's Yvain was quick to call the wild herdsman 'Peasant', even after he gave him information and directions, simply because he was clearly of a low social class. Ser Barristan on the other hand has no qualms about calling a slave and pit fighter 'Ser', a knightly term that in Arthurian legend would not have been lent to anyone but a knight.

Selmy describes his Kingsgaurd vows as 'a sworn brotherhood' with vows 'taken for life… only death relieves us of our sacred trust.'[44] With this in mind, there is no doubt that the character of Jaime Lannister betrayed his Kingsguard vows in 'an utterly unequivocal fashion' by slaying the king he had vowed to protect.[45] Looked at in detail, though, he was still a knight and therefore had the obligation to 'protect the weak and defenceless'. Antonsson and Garcia explain Jaime's ulterior motive in their essay 'A Palace of Love, a Palace of Sorrow: Romanticism in A Song of Ice and Fire'.

'(Jaimie) reveals that part of his motivation was to prevent aerys from destroying the whole city, and all the lives within it, out of some mad belief he'd rise from the ashes in the body of a dragon… Moreover, Jaime knew how the kingsguard themselves responded to Aery's madness, when men like Ser Gerrold Hightower and Ser Jonothor Darry told him his place was to never judge the king, to never intervene if he sought to harm someone, including his own wife, unjustly.'[46]

This backstory makes for an interesting twist when compared with *Yvain* which when put in reference could be seen as a rather simplistic view on what is morally right. Either way, when the reader learns the truth it becomes clear that Jaime is not the villain he was first assumed to be.

The characters in Martin's saga that would traditionally be

---

[44] George R.R Martin, *A Storm of Swords*, (New York, Bantam Books, 1996), P.247

[45] *Beyond the Wall*, P .8.

[46] *Beyond the Wall*, P. 9.

considered villains then, have a depth to the that seems to blur the boundaries of established romance. Even Cersei Lannister, who at all times is put across as cunning and ruthless, is put across by Alyssa Rosenberg as simply 'seeking retaliation for the martial rape and domestic violence to which Robert regularly subjected her in violation of chivalric ideals.'[47] In comparison to Yvain's anti-hero Kay, we have already established that his lack of gravity puts him across more adequately as 'nuisance' rather than 'villain'. Kay does not break the chivalric code, except perhaps ambiguously.

In looking at another character of Martin's, King Joffrey, we see him order his knights to abuse, strip and beat Sansa stark, a girl of twelve.[48] When compared to Chrétien, Martin's characters seem to perpetrate acts of evil completely unheard of in *Yvain: the Knight of The Lion*. 'having his men perpetrate the abuse technically absolves [Joffrey] from direct blame for hitting her, but it also makes the knights complicit in the assault and forces them to choose between obeying his orders and beating a women', this is another true example of the problems inherent in adhering to the chivalric code summed up by Jaime previously. These contradictions though holding much more moral weight are similar to those in *Yvain*, bringing some of the parallels of the two stories to light.[49]

The difference in the depth of character in each work, is a matter for debate. Author Lev Grossman in *Time* magazine declares that 'what really distinguishes Martin, and what marks him as a major force for evolution in fantasy, is his refusal to embrace a vision of the world as a Manichaean struggle between Good and Evil.'[50] This is very fitting when

---

[47] *Beyond The Wall*, P.21.
[48] *A clash of kings*, P.154.
[49] *Beyond The Wall*, P.21.
[50] Lev Grossman, 'George R.R. Martin's Dance with Dragons: A Masterpiece Worthy of Tolkien'
<http://www.time.com/time/arts/article/0,8599,2081774,00.html> [Accessed: 13 Apr 2013] (Para. 6 of 18)

looked at in conjunction with Arthurian legend and Yvain, and is a major difference in analysing the works together. Some other contemporary fantasy medieval writers could be said to keep to a similarly black and white structure of good and evil though, Grossman goes on to juxtapose Martin with Tolkien's *The Lord Of The Rings* bluntly stating that his 'work has enormous imaginative force, but you have to go elsewhere for moral complexity.'[51][52] Grossman's opinion puts lord of the rings on a similar level to Yvain, for the lack of moral complexity we are beginning to outline.

As we can see it is clear from reading Martin's work he does not believe in clear cut heroic characters, it is in this ambiguity that he delivers an interesting idea for a work that is considered in part by Antonsson and Garcia a Romance.[53] The killing of characters that one would traditionally assume to be almost invincible.

Martin's character of Ned stark, one knight that throughout the first book is a close mirror of the chivalric ideal. Taitelbaum although contrasting Tolkien with Martin, allows us an insight in to the Arthurian comparison also. About *A song of Ice and* Fire she outlines how she feels that in the series the 'moral ambiguity mirrors the realities of our world', and that 'those few characters motivated by such obsolete notions as honour or nobility, like Ned Stark, are soon parted from their heads. This "gritty realism" wins praise from genre fans and critics alike, with the implication that, by contrast, Middle Earth is a place of daydream without

---

[51] John .R.R Tolkien, *The lord of the rings*. (Boston: Houghton Mifflin, 1967)
[52] 'George R.R. Martin's Dance with Dragons: A Masterpiece Worthy of Tolkien' (Para. 7 of 18)
[53] *Beyond the Wall* P.6

relevance to our reality.'[54] A daydream place is certainly comparable to Yvain, with the contradicting notions of honour and chivalry. Antonsson and Garcia, however, disagree.

"Gritty," or "Brutal" are terms of reference for many readers when discussing the series, and it can't be denied that these aspects of the story draw a great deal of attention. However, the strength of the novels is not based on literary realism alone. In fact, the realism stands in contrast to another foundational aspect of the narrative: Martin's romanticism".[55]

The ambiguousness of the characters morality is certainly a way to mock the concept of heroism, the fact that these characters are often corrupted or killed is an interesting way to portray how fantasy becomes separate from our archaic notions, Martin's story is less a fairy tale and more a mirror of real life.

In *Yvian,* we see we see lunette rescued at the last minute by Yvain, an example that the innocence of a character can almost become an immunity from harm. In Martin's work however, naivety is no protection. We see this clearly in the character of Sansa Stark, A girl of twelve and daughter to the embodiment of the code of chivalry Ned Stark. She is idiotically unseeing in her assumptions of the world around her and almost blinded by the fantasy stories she read as a child, perhaps they like *Yvain,* forged examples wherein the good prevail and the knights adhere to the chivalric code. She is presided over by Sandor Clegane, a knight who has shaken off his title by his own choice, 'spare me your empty little compliments, girl . . . and your ser's. I am no knight. I spit on

---

[54] Ilana Teitelbaum, 'Decapitating the Chivalric Hero: On "Game of Thrones"', *Los Angeles Review of Books*
<http://lareviewofbooks.org/article.php?id=1543&fulltext=1>
[Accessed: 15 Apr 2013] (para. 8. of 14)
[55] *Beyond the Wall,* P.1.

them and their vows'.[56] Clegane's disillusionment apropos the knightly creed leads him to inform the naïve girl that 'there are no true knights, no more than there are gods. If you can't protect yourself, die and get out of the way of those who can. Sharp steel and strong arms rule this world, don't ever believe any different.'[57] The refusal to accept knighthood and deity together is prominent, especially with the ties to the church we know knighthood had from Kaeupers work in *Holy Warriors : The Religious Ideology of Chivalry*.

Johan Huizinga, the Dutch historian and author of *The Waning of the Middle Ages*, believes that 'for nobles in medieval Europe, tournaments represented the chivalric ideal at its pinnacle'.[58] In *Ice and Fire* Sansa attends one of these tournaments and naturally is taken aback by its beauty and comparison to the stories she grew up on. Jaime Lannister as established is a knight is far from the chivalric ideal, yet Sansa sees him in this way.[59]

According to Ilana Teitelbaum of the *Los Angeles Review of Books*, 'most of us would find it difficult to take the spectacle of a medieval tournament seriously, or not sneer at the code of chivalry (especially knowing what we do about the Crusades).'[60] In fact, it is a credit to Martin that, perhaps exactly because the reader may know the details of the crusades, the event viewed through Sansa's eyes can come across as all the more real. Martin creates a sense of naivety that Chretien never does, regardless of the different stylistic approaches to their work. We know in our hearts that knights

---

[56] *A clash of kings*, P. 39
[57] *A clash of kings*, P. 39
[58] Johan Huizinga, *The waning of the middle ages, a study of the forms of life, thought and art in France and the Netherlands in the XIVth and XVth centuries*. (London: E. Arnold & Co, 1924).p.56
[59] *A game of thrones*, P. 432.
[60] 'Decapitating the Chivalric Hero: On "Game of Thrones'", para 12.

were not the paragons of the chivalric ideal that Arthurian legend puts them across to be and so in not denying us that Martin gives the reader the sense of wonder at the chivalric knight that is perhaps an imitation of the medieval readers feelings.

'Overloaded with pomp and decoration, full of heroic fancy, [tournaments] serve to express romantic needs too strong for mere literature to satisfy. The realities of court life or a military career offered too little opportunity for the fine make-belief of heroism and love, which filled the soul. So they had to be acted. The staging of a tournament, therefore, had to be that of a romance... [61]

Huizinga however does provide that the nobles of the period knew they were not in fact the heroes from Arthurian legend, and in exploring the unattainable standards of the chivalric knight in those texts it is no wonder. Teitelbaum considers the displays as serving 'a real need for romantic expression' and on Huizinga he argues that 'people in medieval Europe were driven by a "quest for the life beautiful" which found its most revered expression in the idea of chivalry.'[62]

Martin's personal opinion on the chivalric code becomes clear in his abundance of characters, from the knight Jaime Lannister to Ser Barristan. In between, we come across what we see as chivalric Knights fighting lesser men and not always coming out on top. For example Martin's crusade against established notions of fantasy writing and the idea of the chivalric code is no clearer than the duel between Sir Vardis, a knight of the eyrie, against the sell sword Bronn. The knight Vardis is in service to a mad noblewoman, Lysa Arran, and in effect fighting for her perverted ends. Bronn is portrayed as a man with no time for compassion or virtuousness, he is

---

[61] *The waning of the middle ages,* P. 57.
[62] 'Decapitating the Chivalric Hero: On "Game of Thrones"'. Para 10.

simply out for personal gain and survival. The battle is drawn out to show how the noble Sir Vardis and his traditional knightly tactics are beaten by Bronn's mercenary style and dirty tactics. As Teitelbaum puts is, 'that final swordthrust to the knight's heart is Martin bringing chivalry to its knees.' She goes on to announce her scepticism that 'that we have then, in the Song of Ice and Fire series, is a cynicism that is not necessarily "realistic" so much as it is a reflection of the author's personal vision'.[63] In some ways this is true, and that 'contemporary readers may like these characters because they are easy to relate to' is certainly, but the reason we can relate to his characters is precisely because they are not put on a pedestal, they are attainable personas.[64] We as readers can imagine ourselves being wowed by a knight in shining armour at a tournament like Sansa is. We can also imagine the hopeless situation portrayed in classic romances, wherein the innocent character or the hero always survives to fight another day, or the knight is the embodiment of the code of chivalry in resisting all temptation. In martin's story though, as in real life, this is rarely the case.

The presentation of weakness in the knight's code of chivalry is an interesting and perplexing one. A Knight is expected to 'Fear god', a virtue we can transfer to *Ice and Fire* in its heavy use of religion throughout. In battle, however, knights were expected to be truly fearless. In Chretien's work we see Yvain proclaim, 'if God will they shall never kill me, nor shall I fall into their hands' to which Lunete replies, 'I shall do my utmost to assist you. It is not manly to cherish fear, so I hold you to be a man of courage.'[65] Fear in general is presented as not befitting a man let alone a knight. This is in sharp juxtaposition to *Ice and Fire* when Ned, who although is to be considered one of the most honourable Knights in

---

[63] 'Decapitating the Chivalric Hero: On "Game of Thrones"' Para 11

[64] 'Decapitating the Chivalric Hero: On "Game of Thrones"' Para 12

[65] *Yvain: The Knight of The Lion*, P.109.

the Saga, is asked by his son Bran, if 'a man still be brave if he's afraid?', 'That is the only time a man can be brave.' Replies Ned.[66]

It could be said the main culprit of the differences between the presentation of chivalry in *A Song of Ice and Fire* in comparison to *Yvain: The Knight of The Lion* is that the reader becomes privy to information that becomes impossible to portray in Chretien's work. They are able to get to know the characters far more intimately, not just because of the series' overall length, but because of the way Martin switches between characters each chapter. This show of the perspective of many characters, many of whom are knights, gives a broader idea of how some men are morally stronger than other in relation to keeping their oaths. In fact, according to Richard Marcus' essay on *A Song of Ice and Fire*, 'Martin is able to use this format to change our opinion of a character. Someone who is depicted as vain, venal, and indolent by others turns out to be far more complex and multifaceted than anyone else ever gave him credit for when we finally meet him.'[67] This is also a means to differentiate between how Yvian can be comparatively uninformative in terms of depth of character.

In fact Marcus's opinion on Ned Stark's adherence to the chivalric ideal is put across as 'so inflexible it blinds him to both the realities of the world he lives in and how others suffer.'[68] As a contemporary reader it is possible to be frustrated by the one-dimensional nature of Ned's moral and

[66] *A game of thrones*, P .9.
[67] Richard Marcus, 'Book Review: A Song of Ice and Fire Series by George R.R. Martin' <http://www.seattlepi.com/lifestyle/blogcritics/article/Book-Review-A-Game-of-Thrones-4-Book-Boxed-Set-2674286.php> [Accessed: 18 Apr 2013]. (Para. 4 of 10)
[68] 'Book Review: A Song of Ice and Fire Series' Para. 5

chivalric code as well as Yvains'. This of course could beg the question of whether or not contemporary readers have the same opinion on the fairness of the code in the first place, maybe they like Marcus agree that Ned's 'simplistic view of the world was unfair and unjust'. Ned however is first described as 'your typical tragic hero', a term that should be in essence a respectable term, however it comes across disdainful. Marcus ends with, 'it's his inability to see the world as anything other than black and white which leads to both his own downfall and the kingdom's descent into civil war.'[69]

The more we look at *Yvain* compared to contemporary medieval fantasy fiction and especially *Ice and Fire* the more we can see it is as Marcus says, of black and white simplicity. It is fairy-tale like, drawing on the archetypes of good and evil in such a blunt way that Chretien's characters are obviously sorted into the categories of irrefutably bad or obviously good.

In contrast, James L. Sutter in his essay 'The Gray Zone: Moral Ambiguity in Fantasy,' pronounces that George R.R. Martin's A Song of Ice and Fire greatness is in its ability to 'remove the boundaries altogether', as 'few of his characters are unimpeachably good or irredeemably evil.'[70] Martin here becomes the embodiment of societal change on literary technique.

[69] 'Book Review: A Song of Ice and Fire Series' Para. 5
[70] *Beyond The Wall*, P.90.

Chapter Three

Examining how Restrictive Conventions Present in the Medieval Era may Affect the Presentation of the Knight's Code of Chivalry in Medieval Fantasy Fiction.

This chapter will explore and if the agendas that were in play during the Middle Ages had an effect on the literature of the era. Specifically religious, societal and political pressures. The effects of all three seem to be intertwined, however, as according to Barber:

The church in the middle ages saw itself as all-embracing, concerned very directly with the humblest of details of everyday life. So, just as the fisherman had his nets blessed or the farmer his seed corn, the knights sword blessed.[71]

This no doubt had a significant impression on any literature to come from the period.

However, this does lead to some problems with how *Yvain* is received as a text portraying medieval life. One could argue that the pressures that imprint on the work seek to make *Yvain* a less then realistic medieval text. Certainly, 'Chretien succeeds in appealing to knight and lady alike, the essential requirement for chivalric literature'[72]. Nonetheless, we have ample evidence that the Knights of the medieval period weren't the saints that the legends of *Yvain* made them out to be. In terms of knightly battle, the siege of Jerusalem during the first crusade gained notoriety as far from the chivalric ideal, described as a 'juxtaposition of extreme violence and anguished faith'.[73] During the siege of Ma'arra, Albert of Aix

---

[71] Richard .W Barber, *The reign of chivalry*. (New York: St. Martin's Press, 1980). P 85.
[72] *The reign of chivalry*. P.112.
[73] Christopher Tyerman, *God's War: A New History of the Crusades*, (Cambridge: Belknap Press of Harvard University Press, 2006)

admitted that that 'the Christians did not shrink from eating not only killed Turks or Saracens, but even dogs.'[74]

The breaking of the knight's code of chivalry as we have established is a major point. A reform after penance, however, is seen both texts to differing degrees. In *Yvian* we see a development of Yvains ideals when he returns from madness and vows to win back his love. He changes from the chivalrous knight gone mad back to the chivalrous knight who claims he will never again forsake his vows. This, as mentioned, is hard to believe. In relation to religious ideals and as a question of penance, the trauma he has endured may not be enough to influence his faithfulness in future. In Jaime Lannister, however, we see a narcissistic, egotistic, murderer of innocents turn into character much closer to the embodiment of the chivalric knight. This however, is similar to *Yvain* as his transformation is only after he loses everything that he holds dear. For Yvian, we are told this is only his love Laudine, yet from examples it is clear he holds his honour far above her. Jaime however, loses his good looks, his fighting prowess, his father's respect and his lover.[75] An enormous penance to pay for a great deal of sin. This change is especially prominent in Jaime precisely because he was considered a villainous character, and through penance Jaime is profoundly changed. He commits some sincere acts of kindness thereafter, rescuing Brienne of Tarth twice from death even though there is great risk for himself.[76]

Sady Doyle, an established feminist critic, writes that

[74] Albert of Aaachen, *Historia Hierosolimitana: History of the Journey to Jerusalem*, trans. Susan B. Edgington, (New York: Oxford University Press, 2007), p. 375.
[75] George R.R Martin, *A Game of Thrones*, (New York, Bantam Books, 1996)
[76] George R.R Martin, *A Storm of Swords*, (New York, Bantam Books, 1996)

'George R.R Martin is creepy, primarily because of his twenty thousand million gratuitous rape and/or molestation and/or domestic violence scenes.' Upon an interview Martin's reply was, 'I have gotten letters over the years from reader who don't like the sex, they say it's 'gratuitous'. I think that word gets thrown around and what it seems to mean is 'I didn't like it.' This person didn't want to read it, so it's gratuitous to that person. And if I'm guilty of gratuitous sex, then I'm also guilty of gratuitous violence, and gratuitous feasting, and gratuitous description of clothes, and gratuitous heraldry, because very little of this is needed to advance the plot.'[77] This is an interesting point, as it seems that the filling out of *Ice and Fire* in 'superficial' details is another way in which it differs from *Yvain*. We cannot compare these adequately though, as there is little information on what Chretien's thoughts about his own subject matter were, we can however say that Chretien was a most probably a religious man. 'All evidence suggests the Chrétien de Troyes was a highly educated man and that he belonged at least to the minor church orders'.[78] George R.R Martin's religious commitments, however, were commented on in an interview:

'And as for the gods, I've never been satisfied by any of the answers that are given. If there really is a benevolent loving god, why is the world full of rape and torture? Why do we even have pain? I was taught pain is to let us know when our body is breaking down. Well, why couldn't we have a light? Like a dashboard light? If Chevrolet could come up with that, why couldn't God? Why is agony a good way to handle things?'[79]

[77] James Lowder, *Beyond the Wall: Exploring George R. R. Martin's A Song of Ice and Fire, From A Game of Thrones to A Dance with Dragons*. (Dallas: BenBella Books, 2012), p.16.

[78] Kirk Mitchell, 'Biography of Chretien de Troyes | List of Works, Study Guides & Essays' <http://www.gradesaver.com/author/chretien-troyes/> [Accessed: 23 Apr 2013].

[79] James Hibberd, 'Interview: George R.R. Martin talks 'A Dance With Dragons'', *Entertainment Weekly*.

The goals of both *Yvain* and *Ice and Fire* are primarily to entertain. Therefore, the reaction of the retrospective audience of both could be said to draw some parallels, few though, as medieval work was undoubtedly charged with certain additional agendas. For example, 'Geoffrey Charney, writing his manual on knighthood in the fourteenth century, saw knighthood and priesthood as the two great orders of the church. Yet originally knighthood was a purely secular arrangement with no religious overtones'.[80]

This blurring of knowledge of the past through external pressures is included in *Yvain: The Knight of The Lion* with Chretien's claim that in the middle ages men 'utter a mockery and lie by boasting where they have no right.' And explaining that in his tale he intends to 'leave those who are still alive, to speak of those of former time.'[81] This idea that things in the past were not quite these authors tell them is highlighted in *A Song of Ice and Fire* and summarised by Adam Whitehead in his Essay 'An Unreliable World: History and Timekeeping in Westeros'.

> '*Samwell tartly suggests that the institution of knighthood is a more recent one and highlights the fact that some stories speak of knights living a thousand years before they could have existed. This is, of course, a nod to the legend of king Arthur, where knights in the medieval tradition are depicted as living and fighting a clear half millennia before such fighting men came into being.*'[82]

This unreliability of stories of the past could be cashed in on substantially, especially by clerics who saw a good

---

<http://shelf-life.ew.com/2011/07/12/george-martin-talks-a-dance-with-dragons/> [Accessed: 15 Apr 2013].
[80] *The Reign of Chivalry* p.112.
[81] Chrétien De Troyes & Burton Raffel. *Yvain:, the Knight of the Lion,* (New Haven: Yale University Press, 1987).
[82] *Beyond the Wall.* P.47.

promotional campaign in the stories spread by bards and minstrels. It would help the spread the stories of knights helped by the grace of god to help promote religion in the eyes of the public. The virtues outlined in *The Song of Roland* give cause to the religiousness of knights, and from the 11th century onwards Bishops would even be present at knighting ceremonies. Knights would now say a prayer to bless them and set them apart as a secular arm of the church.

'O Lord who established three degrees of mankind after the fall in the whole world, that thy faithful people might dwell in peace and secure from all onslaughts of evil, hear our prayers and grant them thy service to use this sword, which by thy grace we bless and give to him and gird on him, to repel the hosts who besiege god's church and to defend himself with thy protection against all his foes.[83]

Being the 'celebrities' of medieval times any trait possessed by the knight would have been seen as a good standpoint on which to base one's own morals. This idyllic version of knighthood was alongside stories of 'Olympic champions, Bedouin poets and Balkan warriors', all of whom could be considered celebrities.[84] This by proxy would encompass the population of young men and children the story reached who would aspire to be more like their heroes. The Catholic church could easily then latch on to this fame for their own ends. This gives reason for the many illustrations of the time that seem to show the knight and religion as a mixed entity (fig 1).[85] The positives of fame for the church are nicely summed up by Simon Morgan. 'The celebrity is a known

[83] Richard W Kaeuper, *Holy Warriors : The Religious Ideology of Chivalry*, University of Pennsylvania Press. (2012) <http://lib.myilibrary.com?ID=421089> [accessed 28 March 2013] (P. 68).
[84] Anderson Kleinberg, 'ARE SAINTS CELEBRITIES?: Some medieval Christian examples', *Cultural and social history*, (2011) v.8 (3) 374-401 (p.393).
[85] *Holy Warriors : The Religious Ideology of Chivalry*. Cover.

individual who has become a marketable commodity. The point at which a public person becomes a celebrity is the point at which a sufficiently large audience is interested in their actions, image and personality to create a viable market for commodities carrying their likeness and for information about their lives and views.' This for Catholicism was certainly true for knights, and putting more and more emphasis on the Knights Christianity was naturally a good way to promote church values.[86]

The *Ordene de Chevalerie* furthers this point, speaking for the churches clerics, it proclaims:

'*knights, . . . whom everybody should honour . . . have us all to guard; and if it were not for knighthood, our lordship would be of little worth, for they defend Holy Church, and they uphold justice for us against those who would do us harm. . . . Our chalices would be stolen from before us at the table of God, and nothing would ever stop it. . . . The good would never be able to endure if the wicked did not fear knights, and if there were only Saracens, Albigensians, and barbarians, and people of evil faith who would do us wrong. . . . it is given to the knight . . . that if he has acted according to his order, he can go straight to Paradise.*'

In this Clerical writers could validate their blessing of knighthood in an openly pragmatic manner. For of course, in the eyes of the church, the chivalric knight was needed to protect clerical property, defend the homeland and suppress or hang heretics. These rationalisations were considered a ruse that simply 'eased the clerical path to sanctified violence'.[87]

---

[86] Simon Morgan, 'Celebrity: Academic "Pseudo-event" or a Useful Concept for Historians?',
Cultural and Social History, 8 (2011), pp. 95–114.
[87] *Holy Warriors : The Religious Ideology of Chivalry*. P. 68.

This violence as a definitive part of the code of chivalry is mirrored in *A Song of Ice and Fire*. At the beginning of the books the upholding of different faiths is presented as acceptable and in that Westeros is religiously tolerant place. That tolerance, however starts to crumble when certain rulers need to use the power of conversion to their own ends. This is further explained in Andrew Zimmerman Jone's essay, 'Of Direwolves and Gods.'

'Stannis barathon becomes a radical devotee of R'hllor, forcing conversion as part of fealty oaths and conquests, and Cersei reinstates the militant orders of the seven, the warriors sons and the poor fellows, which ultimately gain enough power to despose her on their own authority. This trend toward theocratic militarism within westeros had been weeded out in the past and its return does not bode well for the world.'[88]

In doing so, Cersei and the even the rightful king Stannis Baratheon use the chivalric knights sworn to them to further their own ignoble agendas. This again presents the problem of the code of chivalry in as knight sworn to a Lord or King the choice whether to commit act on their whim is a breach of oath in itself. 'Moreover, as great lords themselves, clerics were inextricably involved in the world of armies and knighthood. They held estates owing knight service to some superior lord or to the lord king.' It would not bode well for the enemies of the church with hundreds of knights at the command of the clergy. The clerics themselves 'knew knightly force was needed in a violent and dangerous world and willingly held lands that supported it. Even those without landed endowment necessarily drew on warrior force.'[89]

In *A Song of Ice and Fire*, the lack of the virtue of 'faith' in certain knights is notable. Jaime's transformation, though, gives him a renewed sense of faith. This is in contrast to

---

[88] *Beyond the Wall*. P. 117.

[89] *Holy Warriors : The Religious Ideology of Chivalry*. P. 68.

Yvain's religious mind-set throughout, before, after and even during his madness. When presented with fellow knights faith in the start of the series, one declaring, 'the gods are good', Jaime's immediate reaction is to pity him in his mind, thinking, *'you go on believing that'*. This is not to imply that Jaime is not a pious man, although in not believing that the gods are good, he undoubtedly lacks faith in them. Other characters however seem to clearly doubt the existence of a deity. 'even Asha- as ironborn as they come- laments, 'The drowned god did not answer. He seldom did. That was the trouble with gods.''

When compared with Yvain's consistent piety it is again hard to determine the nature of exactly how he has changed, perhaps this is due to the beliefs that Chrétien held himself. Chretien as a narrator assures in part of the story where Yvain is in the woods that 'the winds dared not blow against God's will'. This could present his characters in light of holding a very biased view on the nature of Catholicism. This when explored seems to be true in the case of practically every character in the story. Gawain even in his persuasion of Yvain to leave his wife brings the Catholic God into his cajoling:

'If I had such a fair mistress as you have, I call God and His saints to witness, I should leave her most reluctantly; indeed, I should doubtless be infatuated. But a man may give another counsel, which he would not take himself.'

Yvain himself is also clearly a pious man, most of the reasoning for what he does is backed up by the pretence that it shall only be done if 'God wills it'. Even when he sets off to leave Laudine he divulges to her he 'would pray God that in His pleasure He may not detain me so long away. But sometimes a man intends speedily to return who knows not what the future has in store for him.'

In *Holy Warriors: The Religious Ideaology of Chivalry*, Keauper has plenty to say about the illustration he uses as the forefront of his book.(fig 1)[90] 'Our illustration, however splendid, is a piece of collusive propaganda. Its visual and verbal program portrays the ideal knight as both pious and fiercely martial, a combination more easily shown in ideal form (as a fight against evil) than could be achieved within the messy details of daily life'. The church can't be solely blamed for this, as although the church would advance this picturesque ideal for knighthood the knights themselves seemed to be 'happy to accept it as a flattering and valorising representation of their profession', and so had no qualms with the public having a far from realistic picture of the reality of knighthood. The picture in essence is 'prescriptive rather than descriptive', a depiction of how the clerics in zealousness wanted knights to be seen, and of course how knights wanted to be seen themselves. 'Yet it would be a great terror to accept this idealized and wishful view as displaying the essence of chivalry; it belongs rather to an effort that flattered warrior sensibilities as it tried to engage warrior piety and direct warrior energies.'[91] Namely, the energies of the knights in protection of the church. As for piety, the grasp the church had on this now not so secular order can be further explained in a much later chapter of Keauper's work, 'Knighthood and the New-Lay theology: Confession and Penance'.[92] The idealised version of the knight the clerics and knights themselves knew to be propaganda could not in reality exist, leading unequivocally to the actual knight being fallible in his aim for absolute righteousness. Therefore the church would give atonement to any sins that may have been committed in return for service, claiming that 'hard struggle would itself become a penance', and, 'killing in warfare (here, of course, the killing of non-Christians)'. The pope further explained that 'killing was permitted when the aim was

---

[90] *Holy Warriors : The Religious Ideology of Chivalry.* Cover.

[91] *Holy Warriors : The Religious Ideology of Chivalry.* P.69

[92] *Holy Warriors : The Religious Ideology of Chivalry.* P.71

repressing crime or fighting enemies of the faith.'[93] This in theory could serve as another reason for justification of the inclusion of Yvain's piety.

'Justice', is clearly in the story of *Yvain: The Knight of The Lion* considered to be a virtue of chivalry on par with that of 'faith'. We see this in Yvain's rescue of the fair maiden Lunette, his questing for penance to make up that of his sin. In *A Song of Ice and Fire*
Thoros of Myr sums up his disillusionment of the virtue:

'Justice. I remember justice. It had a pleasant taste. Justice was what we were about when Beric led us, or so we told ourselves. We were king's men, knights, and heroes... but some knights are dark and full of terrors, my lady. War makes monsters of us all'.

As we have seen from looking at the atrocities committed in the first crusade, it could be deliberated that war was a hugely impactful force in the affecting of a knight's code of chivalry. The knights were intent on claiming this was adhered to, however, it may just not have been suitable for such situations. We know of the trouble Yvain's vows caused him in conflict with his betrothed, we can also look at the contradiction these Knights faced in war. In *From Barbarism to Chivalry*, *name* argues that '*the fighting men, from kings and dukes to simple knights, thought of war not only as an occasional unpleasant necessity but as a worthy and essential occupation and their sole purpose in life.*' Although, in terms of the fantasy fiction genre, we have seen that the idea of courtly love is also integral to the chivalric knight.

This romantic idea of courtly love is similar to the point put across by Antonsson and Garcia in 'A Palace of Love, a Palace of Sorrow: Romanticism in A Song of Ice and Fire' regarding 'the great man theory' in *A Song of Ice and Fire*.

---

[93] *Holy Warriors : The Religious Ideology of Chivalry. P.70*

'Martin's affinity to the theory is less academic and more a matter of pragmatics in storytelling. Readers identify with characters, not socioeconomic trends, so it's natural to position protagonists and antagonists as the primary instigators of events... However, the very act of focusing on the individual as a prime instigator of action falls within the pattern of romanticism established within the series . Characters are quite often directly indicated to be great men.'[94]

This is one societal concept that has not changed since the era of *Yvain: The Knight of The Lion*. Yvain is a indicated to be great man, as is the King Arthur the knights rally for. These similarities show that those pressures inherent at the time of writing have not changed the way the some aspects of fantasy is viewed, with the need to associate great deeds to great men, it is the nature of these epic characters that create epic stories.

---

[94] *Beyond the Wall,* P.12.

Conclusion

From the outset, the aim of this dissertation was to determine whether medieval fantasy fiction of the era of the middle ages was more or less representative of the culture of knights than its same genre contemporary counterpart. This chapter will collaborate the findings on the subject.

The established idea of chivalry in come across in the medieval era romance, *Yvain: The Knight of the Lion*, seems to be directly proportional to how the church, the knights themselves, and society wanted the code of chivalry to be seen. In our contemporary texts, we see the idea of chivalry broken down to solely the authors idea, and although proportional to society's idea for the sake of entertainment, could be argued to be laced with less propaganda.

This in effect is due to the examination of just how little value would have been gained in contemporary fantasy from putting the knights code of chivalry in an uncannily good light, as our of the medieval era text has. We have established that the realism of the Chivalrous Knight in past and present text is still a presentation of fantasy, although as Morrison puts it:

'It has been suggested that romance is an evasion of history... But I am more persuaded by arguments that find in it the head-on encounter with very real, pressing historical forces and contradictions inherent in them as they came to be experienced by writers.'

Considering, this essay has made an effort to argue that the study of the contemporary text *A Song of Ice and Fire* in comparison to *Yvain: The Knight of The Lion* has led to a clear claim that it is more representative of the chivalric knight of the time and, through this, human nature. Primarily, this is due to the dampened effects in the modern environment from political, religious and societal pressures. These pressures have included the egotism of the warrior knight, the objectives of the church and the ambition of its author. In juxtaposition to this, in terms of contemporary work, these same pressures have found to be virtually non-existent.

Martin has been found to be unaffected by the ego of the knight with regards to his period of writing, un-concerning of Catholicism and only really affected by his own ambition in that he includes descriptions thought of by some as 'gratuitous'. This sole aspect being regarded by him as 'not necessary to advance the plot'. Thus in turn this is what presents his work as retrospective of human nature, as, in the words of Alyssa Rosenberg, 'it would be a mistake to suggest that depictions of sexual and domestic violence in *A Song of Ice and Fire* are merely a lurid exploitation'.[95]

My study found the factual accounts of knights of the era very useful in terms of bringing to life the effects of events on the portrayal of the chivalric code. It was impossible, though, to juxtapose this with the chivalric code of knights of the modern era as the knight's code of chivalry seems to nowadays have become obsolete. This limitation could in some way be overcome in the furthering of research into what it means to attain a knighthood in the present day and if the code of chivalry is still in any way adhered to. If I were to partake in this study again, I would include another chapter on idea of the chivalric code of present day knights.

My contribution to knowledge on the subject of medieval literary fantasy fiction would be to argue for the first time on the literary canon of the chivalric code in use in *A Song of Ice and Fire*, and to compare this with Arthurian legend in detail. In particular the comparison to the critics Kaeuper and Teitelbaum.

Further work could be undertaken to establish whether the issues raised in *A Song of Ice and Fire* are present in other contemporary medieval fantasy fiction texts, and to compare them with other works created in the medieval era.

---

[95] James Lowder, *Beyond the Wall: Exploring George R. R. Martin's A Song of Ice and Fire, From A Game of Thrones to A Dance with Dragons.* (Dallas: BenBella Books, 2012), p.17.

Bibliography

Albert of Aaachen, *Historia Hierosolimitana: History of the Journey to Jerusalem*, trans. Susan B. Edgington, Clarendon Press, 2007, ch. V.29, pg. 375

Asbridge, Thomas (2004). The First Crusade: A New History. Oxford.

Baldwin, Marshall W. (1969). A History of the Crusades: The First Hundred Years. Madison, Wisconsin: University of Wisconsin Press.

Barber, R. W. (1980). *The reign of chivalry*. New York, St. Martin's Press. P .112.

Bartlett, Robert (1994). The Making of Europe: Conquest, Colonization and Cultural Change 950–1350. Princeton.

Bouchard, Constance Brittain. *Strong of Body, Brave and Noble: Chivalry and Society in Medieval France*. Cornell University Press.

Chrétien, D & Raffel, B. (1987). *Yvain, the Knight of the Lion*. New Haven, Yale University Press.

Clark, Hugh. "A Concise History of Knighthood: Containing the Religious and Military Orders which have been Instituted in Europe". London, 1784.

Crosland. J. *The Old French Epic*. New York, Haskell House, 1951

Edge, David; John Miles Paddock (1988) *Arms & Armor of the Medieval Knight*. Greenwich, CT: Bison Books Corp.

Edwards, J. C. "What Earthly Reason? The replacement of the longbow by handguns." Medieval History Magazine, Is. 7, March 2004.

Embleton, Gerry. *Medieval Military Costume*. UK: Crowood Press, 2001.

Entertainment Weekly (2011) *EW interview: George R.R. Martin talks 'A Dance With Dragons'*. [online] Available at: http://shelf-life.ew.com/2011/07/12/george-martin-talks-a-dance-with-dragons/ [Accessed: 15 Apr 2013].

Forey, Alan John. *The Military Orders: From the Twelfth to the Early Fourteenth Centuries*. Basingstoke, Hampshire, UK: Macmillan Education, 1992.

Geneviève Hasenohr and Michel Zink, eds. *Dictionnaire des lettres françaises: Le Moyen Age*. Collection: La Pochothèque. Paris: Fayard, 1992.

Gradesaver.com (2005) *Biography of Chretien de Troyes | List of Works, Study Guides & Essays | GradeSaver*. [online] Available at: http://www.gradesaver.com/author/chretien-troyes/ [Accessed: 23 Apr 2013].

Haines, Charles Reginald. (1889). *Christianity and Islam in Spain, A.D. 756-1031*

Keen, Maurice (1984). *Chivalry*. (2005 reprint)

Harvey, P., & Heseltine, J. E. (1959). *The Oxford companion to French literature*. Oxford, Clarendon Press.

Huizinga, J., & Hopman, F. J. (1924). *The waning of the middle ages, a study of the forms of life, thought and art in France and the Netherlands in the XIVth and XVth centuries*. London, E.

Arnold & Co.

Ian, Short (1990). "Introduction". *La Chanson de Roland*. France: Le Livre de Poche. p. 13.
Medievaltimes.edublogs.org (2013) Chivalry. [online] Available at: http://medievaltimes.edublogs.org/chivalry/ [Accessed: 25 Mar 2013].

Kaeuper, Richard W. 2012, *Holy Warriors : The Religious Ideology of Chivalry*. [online]. University of Pennsylvania Press. Available from:<http://lib.myilibrary.com?ID=421089> 28 March 2013. P.168.

Kratins, O. (1964) Love and Marriage in Three Versions of "The Knight of the Lion". *Comparative Literature*, 16 (1).

Laing, Lloyd and Jennifer Laing. *Medieval Britain: The Age of Chivalry*. New York: St. Martin's Press, 1996.

Legends of Camelot (2000) *Chretien De Troyes' Arthurian Romances*. [online] Available at: http://gorddcymru.org/twilight/camelot/chretien/wwcomfort_intro.htm [Accessed: 11 Apr 2013].

Los Angeles Review of Books (2013) *Decapitating the Chivalric Hero: On "Game of Thrones"*. [online] Available at: http://lareviewofbooks.org/article.php?id=1543&fulltext=1 [Accessed: 15 Apr 2013].

Lowder, J. (2012) *Beyond the Wall: Exploring George R. R. Martin's A Song of Ice and Fire, From A Game of Thrones to A Dance with Dragons*. Dallas: BenBella Books, P.16

Kleinberg, A. (2011) ARE SAINTS CELEBRITIES?: Some medieval Christian examples. *Cultural and social history*, 8 (3), p.393.

Martin, G. R. R. (1999). *A clash of kings.* New York, Bantam Books.

Martin, G. R. R. (2011). *A dance with dragons.* New York, Bantam Books.

Martin, G. R. R. (1996). *A game of thrones.* New York, Bantam Books.

Martin, G. R. R. (2000). *A storm of swords.* New York, Bantam Books

Mcconnell, W. (1985) The Dream of Chivalry: A Study of Chrétien De Troyes's Yvain and Hartmann von Aue's Iwein. MLN, 100 (3), p.686-688.

Mills, Charles (2004). *'The History of Chivalry or knighthood and its Times'* Volume I-II
Prestage, Edgar (1928). *Chivalry: A Series of Studies to Illustrate Its Historical Significance and Civilizing Influence*

Read, Charles Anderson (2007). *The Cabinet Of Irish Literature; Selections From The Works Of The Chief Poets, Orators, And Prose Writers Of Ireland - Vol IV* (Paperback)

Robards, Brooks. *The Medieval Knight at War.* London: Tiger Books, 1997.

Sayers, D. L. (1957). *The Song of Roland.* [Harmondsworth, Eng.], Penguin Books.

Seattlepi.com (2012) *Book Review: A Song of Ice and Fire Series by George R.R. Martin.* [online] Available at: http://www.seattlepi.com/lifestyle/blogcritics/article/Book-Review-A-Game-of-Thrones-4-Book-Boxed-Set-2674286.php [Accessed: 18 Apr 2013].

Saul, Nigel. *Chivalry in Medieval England* (Harvard University Press; 2011)

Simon Morgan, 'Celebrity: Academic "Pseudo-event" or a Useful Concept for Historians?', *Cultural and Social History*, 8 (2011), pp. 95–114.

Sweeney, James Ross (1983). "Chivalry," in *Dictionary of the Middle Ages Volume III*
Barber, R. W. (1980). The reign of chivalry. New York, St. Martin's Press.

TIME.com (2011) *George R.R. Martin's Dance with Dragons: A Masterpiece Worthy of Tolkien.* [online] Available at: http://www.time.com/time/arts/article/0,8599,2081774,00. html [Accessed: 13 Apr 2013].

Tolkien, J. R. R. (1967). *The lord of the rings.* Boston, Houghton Mifflin

Tyerman, Christopher (2006). *God's War: A New History of the Crusades.* Cambridge: Belknap Press of Harvard University Press.

Williams, Alan. "The Metallurgy of Medieval Arms and Armour", in *Companion to Medieval Arms and Armour.* Nicolle, David, ed. Woodbridge, UK: Boydell Press, 2002.

Yahoo! (2006) *Courtly Love in French Aurthurian Twelfth Century Romances.* [online] Available at: http://voices.yahoo.com/courtly-love-french-aurthurian-twelfth-century-43660.html [Accessed: 14 Apr 2013].

23814052R00065

Printed in Poland
by Amazon Fulfillment
Poland Sp. z o.o., Wrocław